PRICELESS
Champion of Eventing

Virginia Leng

Compiled and edited by
NANCY ROBERTS

THRESHOLD BOOKS

Published by Threshold Books Limited,
661 Fulham Road, London SW6 5PZ

© Threshold Books Limited 1987

Designed by Eddie Poulton

Typeset by Cylinder Typesetting, London
Printed in Great Britain by Acfords, Chichester

ISBN 0-901366-05-6

To my father, who knew Priceless as a five
year-old, was delighted by his early show of promise,
but sadly never saw him go on to win his Olympic,
European and World Championship medals.

INTERNATIONAL RECORD

	DRESSAGE	SPEED & ENDURANCE		SHOW JUMPING	PLACE
PENALTY POINTS		JUMPING	TIME		
1980 Burghley	44.2	0	27.2	0.5	6th
1981 Badminton	53.2	0	34.8	5.25	8th
1981 Horsens *European*	84.6	0	16.8	0	6th (Team 1st)
1982 Badminton	45.4	0	0	5	4th
1982 Luhmühlen *World*	51.6	0	8.8	0	7th (Team 1st)
1983 Burghley	25.6	0	0	0	1st
1984 Los Angeles *Olympics*	56.4	0	0.8	0	3rd (Team 2nd)
1985 Badminton	59.75	0	0	0	1st
1985 Burghley *European*	49.0	0	0	0	1st (Team 1st)
1986 Gawler *World*	53.8	0	17.6	0	1st (Team 1st)

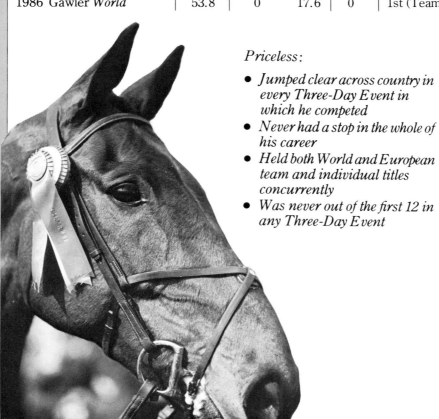

Priceless:

- *Jumped clear across country in every Three-Day Event in which he competed*
- *Never had a stop in the whole of his career*
- *Held both World and European team and individual titles concurrently*
- *Was never out of the first 12 in any Three-Day Event*

Contents

Introduction

This is a book about a superb athlete, a great character
and a loyal friend, and, strangely enough, that
individual happens to be a horse.

Priceless has had a truly remarkable career which has
earned him the affection and respect of everyone who
has been involved with him.

It seems only fitting that some of those people should
join me here to help to tell his story.

Virginia Leng

Early Life

Diana Scott

I bought Priceless's father Ben Faerie in 1970 when he was a two year-old. I was expecting my second child and couldn't hunt, so I was very fed up and decided to go to Ascot sales with my father-in-law to see if I could buy a colt. My husband has always kept stallions to breed tough hunters for Exmoor, and the mares we were usually sent were fairly common, half-bred and less. Knowing this, I wanted to find a Thoroughbred with nice limbs and good looks who would put a lot of quality into that type of mare. I had a picture in my head; he had to be bay with not too much white, and short from the knee to the fetlock, as I believe that many Thoroughbreds today are weakened because they are too long in the cannon bone.

Diana Scott breeds hunters and event horses on a farm high in the Brendon Hills of Exmoor. Priceless was born there and brought on to be a useful hunter. No one imagined for a moment that one day he would be a World Champion . . .

When we arrived at Ascot sales, inside the very first door I opened I saw a gorgeous face looking at me: white star, lovely short limbs; he wasn't very big, only 15.3. And I thought: there's my horse. I only had £250 to spend, but we got him for 240 guineas, and I had to haggle with the lorry driver to get him home because I'd spent all my money!

He went to work as a three year-old and he's never had fewer than forty mares a year, so at a wild guess he must have about 500 children by now. A lot of them are in the hunting field as it was not until Ginny did great things with Priceless and Night Cap that he began to make a name for himself as an eventing sire. He's capable of putting tremendous speed on to a common mare, and although he's the gentlest of creatures, all his children have got immense courage across country as well as a natural eye for a stride when they jump. They don't like to touch anything or knock a fence down and they have an ability to sort themselves out.

Reckless, Priceless's mother, was bought as a four year-old at Exeter cattle market for 125 guineas. It sounds ludicrous today, but then, to a farmer buying a hunter, it was expensive enough. My husband Maurice wanted a good mare to staghunt and liked her bold eye. She was a plain mare, thick-legged and a typical Irish half-bred but she had a flash in her eye and she was a lovely character. Nothing daunted her at all. She had courage with a capital 'C'.

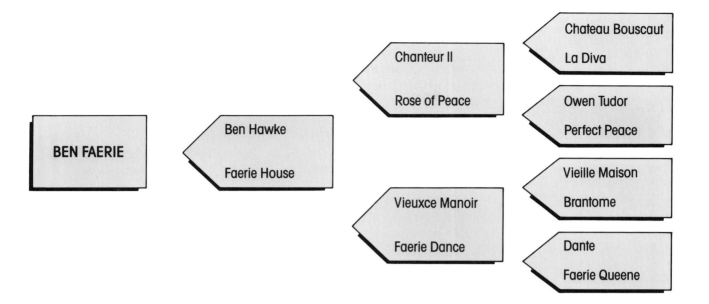

BEN FAERIE

Ben Hawke

Faerie House

Chanteur II

Rose of Peace

Vieuxce Manoir

Faerie Dance

Chateau Bouscaut

La Diva

Owen Tudor

Perfect Peace

Vieille Maison

Brantome

Dante

Faerie Queene

Left: Diana Scott and Priceless, aged four, out hunting with the Devon and Somerset. P. was obviously dependable enough to accompany a pony on a leading rein.

Right: Ben Faerie, Priceless's sire, was bred in Ireland and won on the flat before going to stud. His family tree is shown above. No one knows Reckless's breeding, although she, too, came from Ireland. Compare her expression with P.'s to spot the similarities! Lawless is a full-brother to Priceless and hunts and competes on Exmoor.

Ben Faerie

Reckless

Lawless

9

One day, when I wanted a horse to take to a local hunter trials, Maurice suggested that I should try her. My father-in-law, who had a very dry sense of humour, told me he never opened a gate when he went round the sheep with her: he jumped every one. So I took her up around the back of the farm, jumped three or four gates, and came back glowing with excitement because she had such a marvellous jump. When I told him, Maurice was absolutely appalled; his father had been joking apparently, and Reckless had never jumped a fence in her life! But she went out and won that first hunter trials.

I think Priceless's defiance of life and his bossiness came from her; his brain and intelligence from Ben.

Priceless is a toughy because he was brought up tough. He was born up on The Common, a 70-acre field, under the stars and without anyone in attendance. In those days we foaled out, particularly Reckless, as she hated being inside. He arrived on April 3rd 1973 which was quite early for us, as the grass comes through late here on top of the Brendons. I wish I could say there was something special about his birth – but he just happened. He was not the prettiest of foals, and my sister, when she came over to see him and found him asleep amongst some thistles, said "Oh isn't he priceless!" meaning amusing to look at rather than

The sheds below are the same in which Priceless, along with the other yearlings, spent his first winter at Brendon Hill Farm. Not particularly luxurious, but snug, warm and dry.

Right: P.'s nieces and nephews graze with the cattle in the fields above the farm. Perhaps one of them will follow in his footsteps.

priceless in the money sense. Of course he turned out to be priceless that way too, so I have to give her full credit for naming him.

After he was weaned he spent a winter in an old cattle shed, along with all the other foals, fed well and not kept short of anything. Good quality oats, a bit of sugar beet pulp to dampen the feed and our own silage is what we feed the youngsters, then they don't see an oat until they are in and working as four year-olds. I think this is why they stay sound. Too many people feed far too much concentrate and softening feeds which, I think, can lead to bone problems and weaknesses as the animals grow older.

Priceless must have been one of the soundest horses eventing in his day. He's not particularly big, as we do have a reputation for breeding small horses. We need short-legged horses on Exmoor and I have a theory that big horses are wrong for eventing as they cannot cope as well with bounce fences and such like. Some good small horses have won Badminton, such as Our Nobby and Pasha, and I'm sure they won't be the last.

Priceless was gelded early in his yearling year and then turned out on good grass with just a bit of hay in the winter when it was really hard. He lived out, come hell or high water, then we captured him again as a three year-old to be halter-broken. Otherwise he wasn't

touched at all, except to have the odd worm dose shoved down him, which was a hit and miss job!

He was 'lassoed' as a three year-old because we wanted to show him in hand. I take all the youngsters to local shows as part of their education. We brought him a mile up the road into the stables, shampooed and trimmed him, washed his tail, put a fly sheet on to keep his coat down and bandaged his legs to keep them clean. He was thoroughly tarted up and he didn't think a lot of it! Then he was shut up for the night, ready to leave at six o'clock the following morning. But when we went out next day, the door was open and there was no Priceless. We tracked his bare footprints on the verge and discovered he had galloped a mile down to the other farm, jumped over the hedge back into the field and there he was, grazing quite peacefully, still in his rug and bandages. And could we catch him? Eventually we cornered him, shoved him in the lorry covered in mud, and took him to Brendon show where we scraped the worst mud off and in he went and won his class.

When it came to breaking in, Priceless was taught to tie up first by putting an unbreakable rope halter on him and tying him to a pillar, where he could pull back but wouldn't hurt himself. After that he was handled in the stable and taught to have his feet picked up. When it came to putting a roller on him, I took him over to the cattle shed, popped it on and ran like hell – most of Reckless's children turned themselves inside out when they first had a roller on!

We backed him progressively, putting a bit in his mouth and generally getting him used to us. I like to get on my youngsters and ride them quite quickly, without doing very much lungeing so I started by being led round on Priceless, first in the shed, then up the lane. After that I led him out on the roads in full tack beside another horse to teach him to lead in hand properly. Finally the day came when I jumped on and rode him out with someone leading me.

He wasn't ever a lot of trouble. He was too intelligent and he actually liked going shepherding. On a farm you can't afford to ride round just for the fun of it, so from the day I started riding him I would take him to look at the sheep and cattle, with hound puppies and terriers round his legs all the time. I did practically no flatwork with him. I don't have a lot of time, and anyway I do most of my schooling just hacking round the farm. A horse has to move away from your leg every time you go through a gateway, and every horse at Brendon Hill opens and shuts gates; if it doesn't it soon learns.

I generally ride the youngsters in a rubber snaffle, perhaps with a grakle to stop them leaning on my hands. It's a bit frightening to go out on Exmoor in just a rubber bit and not be able to pull up quickly – in fact it's

The kind of terrain, below, which P. crossed every day taught him to be surefooted and self-reliant. Right: Diana Scott's horses are

perfectly at home with all
the comings and goings of a
working farm — including
hound puppies milling
around the stable yard!

downright dangerous if you see a bad patch of ground and can't stop.

In August that year I took Priceless hunting for the first time. He worked hard that season and did a lot of days and some long hunts but he never once let me down. I think his hunting was one of the things that made him so clever and taught him always to find a fifth leg when he was eventing. We don't jump with the staghounds, but we do cover long distances over very rough terrain with lots of holes and bogs; it takes a hell of a horse to cope with it.

Priceless had enormous ability as a hunter and he loved it. I cracked whips, turned and stopped hounds on him and rode him wherever I wanted to go. As deer naturally work to water, out staghunting you are in and out of rivers all the time and he learned to jump into water without giving it a second thought. I think that has certainly stood him in good stead.

I think that if you treat horses like wimps they'll behave like wimps, so we are quite firm with our youngsters. Priceless was never nasty, and he never bucked me off, although that was a matter of pride to me because I believe that if you are bucked off a youngster, you've half ruined it. However, like all Reckless's children, you could never tell him what to do, you had to *ask* him. If you set about them, then you've got a real fight on your hands, so I was very diplomatic with Priceless.

Catching him was always a problem, and I think if you ask the Holgates, it still is! Like his full brothers, he'd play cat and mouse with me on the worst, windiest, wet day then walk right up to me on the next.

He was never difficult to box, because he used to associate it with hunting, although he did always think he knew it all. One day, after a hard hunt, I was loading him back into the trailer along with a neighbour's horse. As the lady was very elderly, I nipped out of the side door and round to the back of the trailer to give her a hand with the ramp, thinking that the horses were tired and would stay put for a minute. Not a bit of it. Out came Priceless, still in his saddle and bridle, and off he trotted up the road. He quite obviously taunted me when I tried to catch him, letting me get within a yard or two of him, then trotting a bit further up the lane. In the end I drove home behind him, Priceless trotting in front, head up, tail up, occasionally looking back as if to say: 'You can't catch me!'

I was planning to event Priceless at Riding Club standard because he had such a lot of ability out hunting. I had a gut feeling that he was going to be a great horse – but I didn't know then just how great he would be. I never imagined he'd get that chance in life.

Left: Priceless, a gawky four-year old, calm but alert in the hunting field.
Below: The trailer from which he escaped!
Right: Dennis Boyles leads the Devon and Somerset staghounds away from a local meet. Maurice Scott is third from the right.

Competition Life

Virginia Leng

Finding a Three-Day Event horse is rather like looking for a needle in a haystack – particularly as there are no set rules about what should or should not make the grade. It only takes a visit to the veterinary inspection at an event such as Badminton to see exactly how many different shapes and sizes of horse compete there. So it's not surprising that in 1977 when I first saw Priceless I didn't really know what an international event horse *ought* to look like.

In those days my only yardstick was the horses I had seen competing at Badminton and Burghley: champions such as Cornishman, Be Fair, Our Nobby and Columbus, who were all completely different types. Nor were there any great similarities between the three Advanced horses I had already owned. Dubonnet, my first real event horse, was a little 15.2 out of a Dartmoor pony mare. He had taken me to the Junior European Championships, but had only cost us £35! My next mount, Jason, a half Russian Thoroughbred, was an entirely different sort and quite big at 16.2 hands. He had come to us on loan because of a persistent tendency to run away with everyone who rode him. As he had a talent for jumping, we agreed to take him on trial for three months to see if we could break his bad habit. Eventually we succeeded, bought him, and he went on to win the Mini Olympics in Montreal. Tio Pepe, my third event prospect, had been bought by my mother as a yearling. A handsome, pure Thoroughbred, he took me round Burghley, but unfortunately he had tendon trouble and subsequently broke down. This taught us, above all things, that it is essential to find horses with good limbs. Eventing is too testing a sport for any but the fittest.

Thanks to Dubby, Jason and Pepe, my mother and I had well and truly caught the eventing bug, and were enthusiastic, if lacking in experience. We realised that I needed another horse, but the difficulty lay in finding one: particularly as we didn't have a great deal of money and our furniture was rapidly disappearing to swell our funds!

Night Cap, whom we bought as a three year-old from John Chapel, a neighbouring farmer in Devon, seemed a suitable choice, and we felt rather pleased with ourselves. He had good bone, moved well, and jumped nicely. If anything, his stride was a little roundish, but even that was rather a plus point, as knee action can be a tremendous advantage to a jumper when it comes to folding the legs up over fences.

In fact we were so impressed with our new youngster that we decided to go to visit his breeder, Diana Scott, at her stud on the Brendon Hills. My mother in her usual businesslike fashion telephoned Diana to ask if she had any more horses by Night Cap's sire, Ben Faerie. Her reply was a little disappointing. She had nothing of the size we required, and the only one of the right age was her own hunter. However, she invited us to go to see him.

Over the years we have spent endless hours looking at horses. I always rather enjoyed the trips, as they made an interesting break from the routine, and my mother and I would take the dogs, and food for a picnic, and make a day of it. We always felt terribly excited when we set off to see a new horse, not least because we were eager to know if it would be anything like its description. Many a time we've arrived in a state of high anticipation, expecting to see a 16.2 threequarter bred with good bone and no problems, to find a 15.2 heavyweight who weaved and windsucked!

Cornishman, ridden by Mary Gordon Watson. A lovely big horse who was very athletic and could jump like a kangaroo. If he was wrong at a fence he could go straight up in the air if necessary to get himself out of trouble. I think that's why he was so brilliant across country.

Good teeth!

Be Fair with Lucinda Green. A more lightweight type of horse and smaller than Cornishman. He was difficult when Lucinda first got him but despite that he went on to be a real star, which really made him all the more special.

Night Cap. A three-quarter bred, 16.3hh dark brown gelding. Among his best features are his short, strong limbs and good feet. His overall frame from nose to tail is perhaps a little short for his height. Night Cap is a real gentleman at home but he does tend to find 'outings' very exciting indeed — which can cause problems!

Short cannon bones help the tendons to be tough and strong, rather than longer and more elastic.

When the pasterns are short the fetlock joints cannot drop low enough to put strain on the tendons.

What makes an event horse — some of P.'s better points

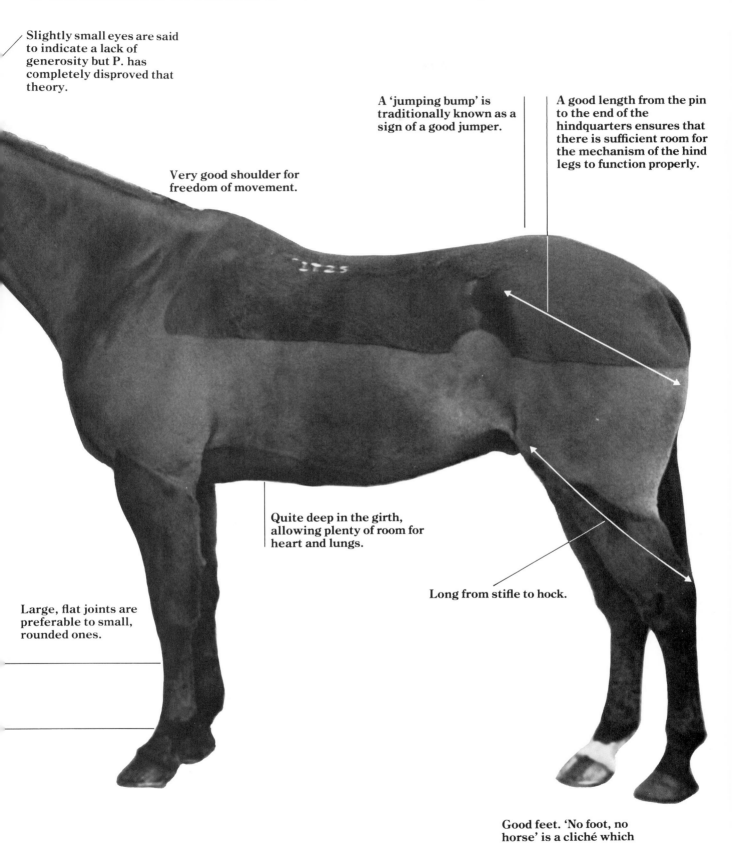

Slightly small eyes are said to indicate a lack of generosity but P. has completely disproved that theory.

A 'jumping bump' is traditionally known as a sign of a good jumper.

A good length from the pin to the end of the hindquarters ensures that there is sufficient room for the mechanism of the hind legs to function properly.

Very good shoulder for freedom of movement.

Quite deep in the girth, allowing plenty of room for heart and lungs.

Long from stifle to hock.

Large, flat joints are preferable to small, rounded ones.

Good feet. 'No foot, no horse' is a cliché which still holds true.

On this particular day, however, we weren't to be disappointed. Diana brought Priceless out of his box and trotted him up for us. His basic shape seemed to fit the bill, and he moved very freely, which we knew would be an asset in dressage tests.

The only slight shadow of a doubt in my mind was whether he would have the stamina to stay the distance of a championship Three-Day Event course. He wasn't terribly big, and he certainly wasn't a Thoroughbred type like Night Cap. However, when I rode him myself, I became more enthusiastic. We popped over a couple of tiny logs and he positively leapt them, with great gusto. He was bold and could obviously think for himself. When buying horses both my mother and I are great believers in following our gut feelings, and we were in total agreement about Priceless. Here, we felt, was a horse worth buying. So, without further ado, we agreed to take him, subject to his passing a vet.

A vetting is always a slightly fraught occasion, as so much hinges on the final decision. This one was no exception, as, for no apparent reason, Priceless had sprung a thoroughpin on one of his hocks. He passed the stringent scrutiny of our vet, Don Attenburrow, with flying colours, but still a question mark hung over the thoroughpin itself. We knew that it could simply be a superficial swelling which would disappear overnight. On the other hand, it might develop into a real problem. We were desolate, until we finally hit upon a solution. We decided to jump Priceless over a nasty, spooky-looking ditch in the field. If he jumped it well, we would take a chance on the thoroughpin. If he stopped, we wouldn't buy him. Looking back, it seems rather a reckless decision, but, notwithstanding, P. sailed over our ditch and we bought him. Fortunately the thoroughpin disappeared as quickly as it had materialised, and thus proved that not every decision should be based solely on technical evidence. Our gut feelings, again, had not let us down.

Priceless settled in very well at Ford, our home in Devon, and he immediately became one of the family. At that time I was going through rather a difficult stage in my career. I had no Advanced horses to ride at all, and having had a taste of the big time with Jason, Dubby, and Tio Pepe, I was finding it difficult to come to terms with having to knuckle down and work with Novices again – particularly as I knew it would be some time, if ever, before I'd get to a Championship competition again.

The two young hopefuls! Priceless and me at our very first unaffiliated competition. Shortly after this photograph was taken I heard an announcement of Lorna Clarke's win at Burghley, and set off on the cross-country course filled with inspiration. Priceless successfully negotiated the first few fences, then shied at some spectators and I found myself sitting on the ground watching him disappear into the distance.

Dorothy Willis

As the Holgates hadn't had very many horses before they bought Priceless, he was a fairly big deal and I was interested to see him. He moved well and it was obvious that he was a 'thinker'. The only trouble is, you can't tell in the early stages whether that's going to work for or against you. So, since he was a stocky, rather heavy-bodied horse who might turn out to be difficult, I said, very stupidly, that I thought he'd make someone a very nice Riding Club horse – and that was about it. Of course it is still true, because he would have done! But through the ensuing years Priceless has taught me one very big thing: the way an event horse is trained is far more important than what he looks like. Most horses, in fact, have got the ability to jump the required dimensions for eventing. The fences are not enormous, compared to show jumping. If the horse moves well and has a good brain then you can do a tremendous amount to develop him. Like an athlete, a horse will get stronger and quicker as he muscles up – and that certainly proved true of Priceless.

Lady Hugh Russell has been a great influence on my cross-country riding and I will always admire and respect her enormously. She is seen here with David Naylor-Leyland, a highly successful competitor himself who is still very strongly involved in the eventing world.

was rather vague about what did or what did not constitute a 'typical' champion, but like Dot, I did know that in my experience few of them looked like our stocky little P. However, there was something about him, and my mother and I were resolved to persevere.

If you look at a photograph of P. as a four-year-old you can understand Dot's feelings. As he still had some maturing to do, his wither was not quite level with his back end, so he gave the appearance of being slightly downhill in front. Because of this he was rather on the forehand, and encouraging him to engage from behind and raise his front end in a more balanced fashion became the chief aim of our schooling work.

To be fair to P., my own lack of experience undoubtedly contributed to his difficulties. I found it exasperating, to say the least, when Pat, after watching my fruitless struggles, would take my place in the saddle and would almost immediately coerce P. into a light and balanced outline. Teaching a horse to be light in the hand, active, and balanced, is a knack, and one that can only be acquired with experience, practice and 'feel'. If I had P. as a youngster *now,* I like to think that I would be able to avoid some of those earlier problems, but it has taken me ten years of perseverence to reach that stage!

Soon after P.'s arrival, Lucinda Green invited me to take him to a Young Rider's seminar which she had organised at Lady Hugh Russell's yard at Wylye. Lady Hugh has been very involved in the training of top eventers for many years, and as this was the first time she had seen P. *and* the first time that he had ever jumped a cross-country fence, it was rather a special occasion. I had done a certain amount of jumping with him, but nothing more adventurous than a few grids and small fences – the usual beginnings for a Novice horse. I was eager to see how he would react to some 'real' obstacles. As I had hoped, Lady Hugh took us up on to the plain, where she had an enormous variety of fences, ranging from the very novice to challenging Advanced combinations. Thanks to her own great experience, she can judge exactly what kind of fences are best for each individual horse, according to his abilities and stage of training. So she simply told me what to jump with Priceless and off we set!

Since P. was still very much a beginner, we were restricted to Lady Hugh's range of 'baby' fences – miniature versions of the kind of jumps you would find on a cross-country course. We jumped most of them from a trot, as they were all very small – but, even so, it was an exciting experience. Priceless showed no sign of being faint hearted, and Lady Hugh was in raptures about his bravery and quick mind. I felt a wave of optimism: perhaps there really *was* hope for him!

However, we aimed to compete with Priceless in the autumn season – which meant that work must begin in earnest. Hunting was all that he had ever done when he joined our yard that spring. Diana Scott had trained him, as she does all her youngsters, by taking him out with the Devon and Somerset hounds. He had learned to lob along calmly in a rubber snaffle, without pulling or yanking or leaning on his rider's hands, so when he came to us he really had no bad habits at all. The steep and rugged Exmoor terrain had also taught him to look after himself; to travel fast, up and down hill and to splash in and out of streams and rivers without a moment's thought. It had been a wonderful start for a potential event horse. Now I needed to concentrate on slow flatwork, teaching him to move correctly in a rounded outline for the dressage phase; as well as introducing some jumping training.

To ensure that we were working on the right lines, we took P. along with Night Cap for some sessions at Pat Manning's yard in Reading. Pat and her assistant, Dorothy Willis, had been a great deal of help to me in my Junior days and I relied on their opinions enormously. Pat liked P. but was rather non-committal about his potential as an international eventer. Even less encouraging was Dot's opinion. She thought he was *desperate!* He would make a good Riding Club horse, she suggested — which, considering his appearance at the time, was a fair enough judgement. I

P., however, wasn't about to let everything be such plain sailing. He chose that seminar to demonstrate a very unfortunate habit which has remained with him all his life. He bucks, and he bucked with embarrassing regularity throughout our dressage sessions. It first happened while Bridget Maxwell, our coach, was riding him herself in order to demonstrate a point to me. She asked him to canter, and he bucked. So she gave him a little tap with her stick – nothing more, just enough to say 'No'. He bucked again, and Bridget hit him again – and so it went on. Priceless would not give in, but eventually Bridget *did*. 'Right,' she said, 'We won't hit him.'

Every time I asked him to canter during those sessions, he bucked. We ignored him, and by the end of the week he had stopped doing it. That was an important lesson I learned about P. He is the sort of horse who will not be told what to do. He likes to do things his way, and if you try to boss him he will never give in. I believe that it's such self confidence – almost conceit – that has made him famous. But in order to make it work for *me,* I realised that I'd have to learn to outsmart him. I'd never be able to get the better of him by bullying.

P. was five when I took him to his first competition, a Novice One-Day Event at Henstridge. It was a lovely day, the sun was shining, and he jumped a very good clear round. I was thrilled. Lucinda had watched him go, so I asked her what she thought. 'He might be all right', she replied, in a slightly guarded fashion. It was a difficult question, and *I* didn't know the answer to it. Whether Lucinda wished to hazard an opinion or not, she certainly didn't want to discourage me. But nonetheless I was optimistic. There was nothing to lose. So I decided 'If I'm wrong, I'm wrong, and that's just too bad.' In retrospect, poor P. had a great weight hanging on his shoulders – the burden not only of my inexperience, but of my whole future.

At the time, Night Cap and Priceless were coming along side by side. To all intents and purposes they seemed equally promising. If anything, N. might have looked the better prospect – he is certainly a much more attractive, quality type of horse than the rather butch and workmanlike P. But, funnily enough, I never doubted that P. would come out on top.

His second event that autumn was Taunton Vale, and that was where we had our hiccup: the one and only mistake he has ever made in his whole life. I think he'd got the bit between his teeth, as they say, and had started to think that this eventing lark was all rather fun. He was still wearing a rubber snaffle, but I was finding him very strong. As we headed downhill towards a double of rails, with P. pulling hard, I said: 'Whoa, steady, steady, whoa'. But I was talking to a pair of deaf

ears, and we missed our stride going into the fence. We had a choice of either one long stride or two short ones. P. tried for something in between, and didn't make it. He literally cartwheeled over the first element of the fence, catapulting me into the second part with such force that it promptly broke. It was a pretty hefty fall, but we picked ourselves off the ground. I got straight back in the saddle and we carried on. P. wasn't in the least bit upset. He just shook himself, seemed to say: 'Fair do's' and then, without a qualm, put it out of his mind. 'Right. Come on – let's get on with it,' appeared to be his attitude. After that, he listened to me more, but he wasn't at all perturbed. It's not in his make-up I think, to be perturbed by such things, and that has been his attitude throughout our career.

In spite of our difficulties on the flat at home, P. went beautifully in his dressage tests at those early events. Apart from the slip at Taunton Vale, his jumping also was brilliant and seemed to come quite naturally to him. He was so quick, clever and surefooted that we really didn't have to teach him anything. Even as a Novice, when a few mistakes can be put down to experience, he never once hit a fence hard in front. That, in fact, remained true for the rest of his career. He never stopped and he never made a bad mistake, yet in his eight years of competitions he must have jumped literally thousands of fences. It is quite an extraordinary thing to be able to say about any horse.

Our first win together was a Novice class at Tetbury. This was followed by several Intermediate outings, until in 1979, when P. was six, we decided to enter him for the Bramham Three-Day Event. It was a big step for him. I remember that outing rather well, because I hadn't done a Three-Day Event for two and a half years, and I was very nervous about it. All my usual worries about the steeplechase and getting lost on the roads and tracks were doubled. The fact that I was riding a very inexperienced horse doing *his* first Three-Day Event made things even worse. I remember watching other competitors on the steeplechase for hours, just to remind myself what I was supposed to do. I think I walked and drove round the roads and tracks about fifteen times.

On Day One, P. had the best dressage score, which was heartening, and put us in the lead for the speed and endurance. Yet I knew from experience that the real test was still to come.

That cross-country day was something of a trip into

A relaxed moment for Priceless and me. At that time he had a splint on his near fore but luckily he was never lame and the unsightly lump has now disappeared completely.

Bramham Three-Day Event. Priceless athletically clears the final element of the Coffin, in spite of the fact that I had ridden the first part so badly!

the unknown for me. I didn't really know what sort of a horse I'd got or how he'd react to the different phases and the greater distance. It was far longer than the One-Day Events we were used to. Anything could happen.

Despite my concern, P. enjoyed the steeplechase. In preparation, we'd had a school over a couple of fences on a farm near our home in Devon. He seemed to get the hang of it, so on the day, I just decided to crack on. And we did. In spite of my hours of deliberation over the cross-country course, however, things didn't all go according to plan. Near the start, coming into a difficult coffin, I completely missed my stride. Missed – with a vengeance. I buried poor Priceless into it! Any lesser horse would have come to a grinding halt, but dear P. – goodness knows how – managed to extricate himself. We struggled through, and continued on our way, miraculously without a fault. Funnily enough, after that, I relaxed. The very fact that he could so easily have stopped, but didn't, made me realise that here was a horse so brilliant that even if I did make a pig's ear of something, he would rescue me.

As P. had gone clear, we maintained our lead at the end of Day Two. The following afternoon we suffered a slight setback in the show jumping, when we had a fence down: a rare occurrence for P. who was, and always has been, a very careful show jumper. As it

happened, it didn't matter, as the horse lying second had a fence down too, so we still came first. That night we threw a party in our caravan and my boss, Jeremy Hamp, whose video company I had worked for during the long winter months, presented me with a Champagne cork which had a 50p piece pressed into its stem. It was a lucky charm, I was told, and I've carried it in my hat box ever since. I really do believe that cork has brought me a great deal of luck over the years.

Of course it's always exciting to win, but for me this particular event meant even more than usual. In my eyes P. had proved himself. Before, I had been just a little dubious about his strength and stamina, and though I wouldn't have admitted it to anyone, I had wondered in my heart whether he really was capable of tackling a Three-Day Event successfully. The moment he won Bramham I was convinced. Not everyone felt the same as I did, but that didn't matter. As far as I was concerned P. had everything required of a champion. All he needed now was a little more confidence and a little more time. I was sure he was going to be a star.

Our win at Bramham also helped me decide whether or not I should continue with my chosen sport. Having spent a great deal of my parents' money, as well as my Uncle Jack's – since he, too, had helped finance us for seven years – I felt that perhaps at last we were going to get somewhere.

Roads and Tracks

An asset to horses during the speed and endurance test of a Three-Day Event. Phase A, which covers four to six kilometres at a fast trot or a slow canter interspersed with a little walking, is an excellent warm up for the steeplechase. Phase C normally covers twice the distance and helps the horse's heart and respiratory functions to recover before the cross-country.

Steeplechase

Similar to a National Hunt racecourse, Phase B is a grass track between two and two and a half miles long with ten fly fences to be ridden at a gallop. The aim is to complete the course without time penalties whilst conserving as much of the horse's energy as possible.

Cross-Country

Accuracy, boldness and rhythm are the key factors to a good round. If you can achieve these you are well on the way to the thrilling experience of true harmony between horse and rider.

The dressage phase of a Three-Day Event tests the horse's paces, balance and obedience with a series of set movements in an arena. These might include medium and extended paces, circles, serpentines, rein back, half-pass and counter canter. The panel of judges award marks out of ten for the way in which each exercise is executed, and convert the final score into penalties. The fact that the horse must be fit enough to tackle the second day's cross-country presents an added difficulty for the rider. Priceless, for one, would often be so bursting with energy that he found it hard to concentrate on the precise disciplines of the test.

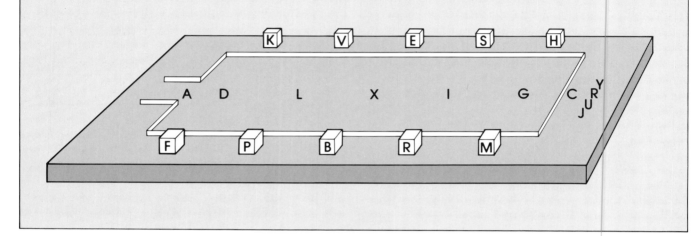

I had begun that year with two Intermediate horses and finished it with two Advanced ones, which was a very satisfactory state of affairs. Not only that: Priceless and Night Cap had upgraded so quickly that they had actually been able to compete in Advanced classes that same year, without having to wait until the following season to take the plunge. They were still only six year-olds – which is young for an Advanced horse – but I felt convinced that they were ready for it.

Based as we were in Devon, we didn't have a great many competitions to choose from, but P. and N. still had nine or ten Novice events plus several Intermediates behind them before they competed in their first Advanced competition at Tetbury. That autumn they also did the Advanced section at Chatsworth, a big course and quite a lot to ask them but we had already spent some considerable time at the back of the field. Now we thought we'd kick on and see what happened. It was wonderful when both P. and N. jumped well and clear in their Advanced classes, and we went home thinking that we actually had two quite nice horses!

During this time I was taking Priceless to Pat Manning's as often as we could afford it. Every six weeks or so, my mother and I would set off for Reading with our two horses, and a caravan to save on accommodation bills. We worked hard. As well as looking after my two, I'd muck out stables for Pat, to earn extra lungeing lessons. But I enjoyed our trips there enormously, and certainly learned a great deal.

Pat has given me a thorough grounding in dressage over the years, as before I went to her I really didn't understand it. She thought that Priceless was very smart and had a good brain, but she was perceptive enough to point out that we'd have to be careful how we treated him. If we tried to do too much he was the kind of horse who would easily become stale. In those days we didn't have an outdoor school at home, so even if I'd wanted to, I wouldn't have been able to do very much dressage there. If we were lucky and the weather was on our side, we'd fit in a couple of schooling sessions a week at the most, and that included jumping as well. We did a lot of road work, and would ride out, up and down the local hills, for hours at a time to keep him fit.

Nowadays, with an outdoor school, we do at least four days schooling a week, and if Priceless came to us now as a youngster we'd train him in a totally different way. He'd be schooled much more frequently and would perhaps have more jumping sessions to improve his technique – not that I'm convinced he'd be any the better for it. Sometimes ignorance *can* be bliss, and too technical a régime might have spoilt his natural talent. I just don't know.

Our second Three-Day Event was in Holland the following spring, at Hooge Mierde. Although it meant a trip abroad it was just the right standard for both Priceless and Night Cap: a little more difficult than an Intermediate but not as testing as Badminton or Burghley. There aren't many events like that to choose from, which is why we decided it was worth the journey.

I had competed abroad before, as a Junior, but not for some time, so it was quite an expedition for all of us. Uncle Jack, who part owns Priceless, came to watch, and my mother drove the horsebox. We made the crossing by ferry, and P. who always travels well, arrived very fit and very excited about the whole thing.

The cross-country course was beautifully built: far better than we had expected. The dressage arena was set in a little clearing in the woods: a most attractive backcloth as far as the riders were concerned, but from the point of view of a horse it was, most certainly, quite spooky. No call, however, for P. to behave as badly as he did! Like a small child at a party he became completely over-excited at the novelty of the occasion.

I did everything I could think of to quieten him down. I worked him in, I took him for a long hack, I even whistled and sang to him. I've never been a particularly good singer, so perhaps that was the final straw; but once we got inside the boards of the arena he found the atmosphere just too much to handle. Even before we'd started doing anything of a serious nature he had put in a couple of bucks, and he then proceeded to perform one of the most interesting tests of his career. He bucked and kicked and squealed. He added levades, flying changes and a turn on the haunches, none of which, unfortunately, figured in that particular test. Only by the skin of his teeth did he manage not to come last. Night Cap didn't behave a great deal better, but he was certainly not quite as bad as P.

Having been in the lead after the dressage at Bramham, I felt that Priceless had rather let the side down. Fortunately he made up for it by giving me a super ride on the cross-country the following day. However, that was not before another hiccup: this time on the steeplechase. The course was set in a figure of eight, which I find confusing at the best of times. On this occasion I lost my way altogether. While I dithered, we had to grind to a halt, which must have been most disconcerting for P. quite apart from the fact that every second, literally, counted. I don't know to this day how we managed to get within one second of the optimum time, once I'd finally set off on course again!

The cross-country included several natural ditches, which are used by the Dutch for irrigation and which can confound horses who are naturally suspicious of water.

**P. and me
at Locko, 1980.**

27

Not P. however, who, thanks to his days on Exmoor had always been a very good ditch jumper. His round boosted our position up twelve places to a much more respectable 12th, and we came home well satisfied that we hadn't disgraced ourselves after all. I wasn't to know then that this would be his lowest placing ever in a Three-Day Event!

As P. had become more confident and was now too strong for his rubber snaffle, I had been trying to find a satisfactory substitute bit which would give me rather more control across country without inhibiting him. One answer had seemed to be a gag with two reins, so that I could ride on the ordinary snaffle rein and only fall back on the gag action in moments of stress. I used it for about eight months but eventually decided it was rather too strong for him, so switched again to a Dr. Bristol, in which he has gone happily ever since.

I tried various bits for his dressage, as well, including the traditional double bridle, but finally concluded that he went best in the snaffle and grakle noseband which I use for schooling at home.

After Hooge Mierde the next target for P. was Burghley, in the autumn of 1980. Although he had competed in a few advanced One-Day Events, this was still an enormous step for him. Burghley is one of the most testing courses in the world, and attracts the greatest horses, but there was no earthly reason why Priceless shouldn't attempt it. So far he had done everything we had asked of him.

Shortly before we set off for Lincolnshire I took P. cantering in a new pair of brushing boots. I returned to the stables to discover that in the process his legs had been rubbed quite raw. The next few days were a complete horror as I waited on tenterhooks to see if his legs would swell – in which case Burghley was as good as forgotten – or would heal in time for the event. But P. is a born toughy: the rubs mended straight away, and off we set.

Once we'd arrived I began to wonder why I'd been so eager to get there in the first place! The cross-country course was certainly one of the biggest I'd ever seen. I walked it again and again until eventually I had worked out a route through the fences which I thought would be within our capabilities and wouldn't stretch P.'s confidence too far.

Fortunately, this time there were no ghosts in the bushes to divert P. during his dressage. In the months since Hooge Mierde I had become rather more wise to him, and had formulated precise tactics for working him in beforehand. It was essential not to do too much concentrated schooling, as P. would quite quickly develop a glazed expression, lean heavily on my hands,

This photo clearly shows the two-rein gag bit which I used for a while on Priceless. I found it rather a nuisance, though, and shortly afterwards switched to a Dr. Bristol, which proved to be a happy compromise for horse and rider.

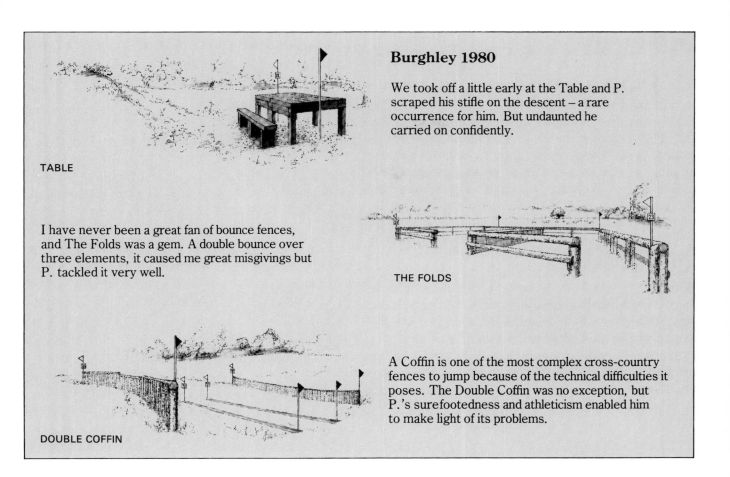

TABLE

Burghley 1980

We took off a little early at the Table and P. scraped his stifle on the descent – a rare occurrence for him. But undaunted he carried on confidently.

I have never been a great fan of bounce fences, and The Folds was a gem. A double bounce over three elements, it caused me great misgivings but P. tackled it very well.

THE FOLDS

A Coffin is one of the most complex cross-country fences to jump because of the technical difficulties it poses. The Double Coffin was no exception, but P.'s surefootedness and athleticism enabled him to make light of its problems.

DOUBLE COFFIN

press his ears against his skull, and generally look bored out of his mind; not a great help when you are about to enter the dressage arena with the intention of conveying impulsion, activity and obedience in all paces. So at Burghley, I tried very hard not to overdo our warm up, restricting it to thirty or forty minutes at the most. Instead I took him for a walk around the grounds to get him used to the crowds and the tents and all the usual silly nonsenses which are part and parcel of a big event. Not that he found that kind of thing upsetting: in fact he has always seemed to consider an audience his God-given right; but I knew that if he was feeling fit and excited and had no outlet he would look for an *excuse* to misbehave. I had to try to prevent him displaying that fitness and freshness in the place where it was most unwelcome: namely the dressage arena. Once I'd learned how to do that, P. didn't often behave badly, and on this occasion he did such a good test that we were lying in first place at the end of the first day.

As it was P.'s first visit to Burghley, and only the second time that I had ridden there, the cross-country was rather a matter of trial and error for both of us. Everything went smoothly, apart from one heart-stopping moment, when I saw an incredibly long stride to a large shark's teeth fence with a very big spread, but

P. proved his tremendous scope and sailed bravely over it. We went clear, but as I didn't ride particularly confidently we finished with quite a few time faults. It didn't concern me in the least; I hadn't dreamed of finishing inside the time on such a big course. I was never particularly a speedy person and at Burghley all I wanted was to go clear, do a good job, and make our round look fluent and comfortable. If P. went well and finished feeling happy we could always go a bit faster next year. In fact we ended up in sixth place – which was more than I'd ever hoped for in view of our time faults. That night, however, as we all celebrated madly, two people, quite separately, expressed the opinion that although P. had ability, in their view he had neither the class nor the blood to be able to really gallop so would never make an international horse. No one could have found a better way of deflating me at that precise moment, but I was determined to stand by P. Maybe he wasn't a Thoroughbred, but I was sure that there were ways and means of picking up time, and I knew that we both needed to gain confidence. One day, I convinced myself, we would finish without time faults. It wasn't that I knew P. was capable of it, because truly, in those days, I didn't know. But I was so proud of him that I would have done anything to defend his reputation. I was determined to prove a point.

That winter we thought carefully about the way we were getting P. fit. Was he perhaps too fat? Up until then we had religiously followed the precepts of a book on interval training written by the American rider Bruce Davidson. Now we began to wonder if this was, after all, the best approach for P. Interval training concentrates on sustained lengths of canter work to increase fitness, which P. found both boring and physically undemanding. We talked to trainers, studied different systems, and decided to try a different method to get P. ready for Badminton. We started him on a new régime of short, sharp bursts of work similar to the programme followed by many racehorse trainers. We also put him on a strict diet. We were aiming to build him up into the lean yet muscular physique of a racehorse, which we hoped would put him in the best shape for the demands of a Three-Day Event. He certainly found the work less boring but he was totally unimpressed by his diet!

It was while we were getting P. fit and ready for Badminton 1981 that we discovered he didn't like jumping at home. He found it boring, and if we persisted then he'd start to jump flat and generally refuse to take things seriously. Regular schooling and grid work can improve or alter the way of going of most horses. But not P. He had his own style and he was sticking to it. As a precautionary measure, to reduce the risk of tipping a pole in the show jumping phase, I was keen for him to round up a little more over upright fences. This preoccupied me for several months, as I racked my brains to think up ways to persuade him to do so.

After discussions with Pat Burgess and Dot, I tried putting a placing pole nine or ten feet from the fence to make him take off closer. This, I reasoned, would mean that he'd have to round up to jump cleanly. Instead, P. cunningly put his feet so close to the pole on the ground that he was no nearer the jump than before. Jumping him down a tight grid didn't work either. My intention was for him to land so near to each successive jump that he would be forced to pick up over it. But he foiled me again. He took such incredibly short strides between the fences that he could stand off just as far as before. I was reduced to tears of frustration more than once, while P. in turn got more and more cross, so in the end I said: 'Why bother?' and I gave up. He always jumped clear rounds unless *I* did something wrong, so it seemed pointless to persist. Instead, I took him indoor jumping during the winter, which he loved. He actually qualified for regional Foxhunter finals about five times, but we were never able to take him further, as they were always held in the summer when the eventing season had started again. Perhaps he could have been a great show jumper: Ted Edgar, whom we used to meet quite

Priceless stands well back from the notorious Aintree fence during our first ride at Badminton in 1981.

Jumping towards P.'s first win at Locko Park: the Midland Bank Open in 1981.

31

regularly on the indoor circuit, certainly liked him, and often offered to take him off our hands!

In October 1980 we moved from Devon to Acton Turville, a little Gloucestershire village only a few miles from Badminton House. The fact that our new home, Ivyleaze, was closer to civilisation, meant that we had much less travelling to do in order to reach our competitions. As we have a day's work ahead once we arrive at an event, this was a huge advantage, and also cut down our travelling expenses. With Badminton on our doorstep I could now enjoy the novelty of actually hacking P. to Britain's premier event, instead of having to load him into a lorry and drive several hundred miles.

However, Badminton's proximity did nothing to lessen my awe for it. The name sends shivers down my spine, and though each year I try to convince myself that the course cannot really be as big as I think it will be, unfortunately it always is!

That first look at a cross-country course, when the riders walk from fence to fence assessing the problems at each, is, I think, the nearest we can get to seeing the course through our horses' eyes. *They* never get a chance to look at the obstacles before they have to tackle them – at speed – and it is a great test of their courage and trust.

At Badminton, I had my first attack of bravery. I was beginning to get to know Priceless, and ventured a few quick routes through fences on the cross-country which a year before I wouldn't have tried. He finished eighth, with ten time faults, which was very respectable, and we were chosen to ride for the British team in the European Championships at Horsens, Denmark.

Locko Park was the final selection trial for Horsens and it had always been a great ambition of mine to do well in the Open Championships there, at that time sponsored by the Midland Bank. It was also an opportunity for me to meet and personally thank some of the members of the Horse Trials Support Group. This marvellous band of people give invaluable financial help to young event riders, and had that year ensured that I could continue to train with Pat Manning. These were the days before my British National Life sponsorship and I was indebted to them for their support.

Locko turned out to be a great success, as P. managed to win the Open. Not without a certain amount of amusement in my dressage test though, for I entered the arena, halted, saluted and looked down to find my pink and white knickers staring back at me. In my haste to change from one horse to another in the collecting ring my flies had come undone! The judges unfortunately had also noticed. It was causing them enormous amusement, which increased as I carefully and deliberately did up my breeches before carrying on.

About this time, Dorothy Willis came to join us at Ivyleaze. She had been helping us at events quite regularly, as well as visiting us in Devon on days off and holidays, so when she left Pat Manning's yard to go freelance she started to come to Ivyleaze three days a week. After Badminton, she moved in altogether, and she's been here ever since. I don't know what I would have done without her during the ensuing years.

Horsens was my first time in a senior team, and I was absolutely delighted to be selected. It was all I'd ever wanted to do, and was the realisation for my ever-supportive mother and myself of years of striving. The girls in our yard at the time were still relatively inexperienced, but the 'Powers that Be' insisted that a groom, rather than Dot or my mother, should accompany P. on the journey, so we had to look for some outside assistance. Karen Priddy Smith was recommended to us, and agreed to help out. To get to know P., she came to work at Ivyleaze, then travelled with him to Horsens and back. A groom at an international event has a very responsible job. She is answerable to the Chef d'Equipe, the official vet and, of course, the rider! She also needs to know her horse and his routine well enough for him to be disturbed as little as possible by the journey and the unfamiliar environment, and Karen was exceptional in every way.

P., unflappable as always, travelled very well and, thanks to his rather ferocious nature, was billeted in the end stable of the British team block to act as guard dog!

When we set out to walk the course it was slightly alarming to find that the cross-country was the most difficult that – even to this day – I think I've ever seen. As it was my first experience of a championship course, I couldn't then make comparisons, so I didn't have a clue how bad it really was. All I knew was that it frightened the life out of me! Nor was it encouraging to find that my far more experienced team-mates, Richard Meade, Sue Benson and Lizzie Purbrick, shared my feelings. I'd imagined Horsens to be flat, but the organisers had managed to find a hilly part on which to build the course. And what hills! Some of the approaches to the fences were so steep that we could barely negotiate them on foot. I was close to tears at the prospect of attempting what seemed the impossible, but Richard was rather more optimistic. 'Don't worry, they'll have to lower them,' he said, and he was right. The teams petitioned and we all met up for a Champagne party at the notorious Fence 13, to celebrate its reduced height.

Burghley 1980. The Table was one of the obstacles that concerned me. The main difficulty at this massive spread was the approach down a steep bank, which gave riders little chance to present their horses in balance. Priceless took off early and cleared the fence with his front end but caught his stifle on the way down, luckily without causing serious injury. The expression on his face here shows his determination and guts.

Midland Bank Championships, Locko Park 1981. An unusual shot of P. galloping between fences. Note the tail in action and the look of concentration on his face.

Luhmühlen 1982. Flying over a parallel of maximum height and spread. P. always jumped this type of fence aggressively which gave me great confidence.

Horsens — and an impressive spread fence sited at the bottom of a near vertical descent. The steepness of the approach obviously added to the difficulty of the fence, and it claimed a number of victims.

I was still not looking forward to the cross-country, particularly since our Chef d'Equipe, Malcolm Wallace, had picked me to go first for the team. This didn't strike me as the best idea in the world, as the least experienced member of a team usually rides second rather than being the trail-blazer, but Malcolm thought a lot of Priceless and felt that we could cope. Then we discovered that not only was I Number One for our team: I had also been drawn first to go out of the whole field.

To make matters worse, Horsens was blanketed in a thick fog, and I had to ride my dressage test in a pall of mist. I have no idea how the judges saw me as I certainly couldn't see them!

The night before the cross-country I didn't actually sleep very well and I woke to thick fog again, which didn't improve my mood. By half past six I was out checking P.'s equipment and putting on his bandages and studs.

As the first to go, I obviously didn't have the opportunity to see how other riders fared on the course, so I had to make my own decisions about which routes would be best. We took what turned out to be the shorter, 'brave' routes at all fences except one, the Horsens Bridge. This was a small platform with a take off rail and a huge ditch behind it. When walking the course I'd noticed a water jump on the steeplechase that was very similar to it: a small brush with a big spread. I'd said to myself then that if Priceless stood off the water jump on the steeplechase he would doubtless stand off the Horsens Bridge on the cross-country phase. If he did, we would come to grief by being *too* bold, because he would land into the face of the bank on the other side instead of clearing it.

Sure enough, on the steeplechase, where we had to jump the water twice, he stood off both times. This made my mind up, and I chose the alternative, slower route, at the Bridge. Fortunately, by the end of the day I had been proved right; every horse who stood off at that particular fence fell. Only the ones who went in close managed to clear it.

I wouldn't like to have attempted that course on many horses. In fact I don't think I'd like to have attempted it on *any* other horse. But I knew that Priceless was intelligent enough in his approach to fences to be able to deal with all the situations which arose.

I certainly thanked God that P. had hunted on Exmoor and that he knew what it was like to go up and down hills, because at some stages the terrain was so steep that we were forced to slow to a walk. It was particularly difficult because the ground was very variable which can also upset some horses.

I was dreading one fence in particular: a downhill bounce which was a very big upright of white railings

across a road, with a bounce stride out over a second set of railings and a huge drop on the landing side. It was a real pig, and there was no alternative route. I'd once had a crashing fall with Tio Pepe at a bounce, because I came in too fast and he'd tried to jump both elements together. I've never liked bounces since, and that fence at Horsens caused me nightmares. Priceless got me through it, though, and jumped it very well.

As it turned out, his round was the best of all the British horses, and our team won, with P. and me sixth individually. That, I felt, was a turning point for P. – his first International Team Championship.

Our new fitness programme was obviously working and at the end of the season P. was slimmer and fitter than he'd ever been before.

Badminton 1982 – the Irish Bank which, many years before, one competitor, John Shedden, cleared in a single leap.

Having been successful in Denmark we thought we'd be in with a good chance for the team to go to the World Championships at Luhmühlen – as long as P. went well at Badminton. In fact he was fourth *and,* by cutting corners and taking the bold, short routes over fences, he finished inside the time across country. In the early days at Burghley eighteen months before, I might not have been able to foresee such total brilliance but at last

I felt that my faith in P. had been vindicated. This time, no one could say he wasn't fast enough!

Unfortunately, in the show jumping phase P.'s quick reactions were my downfall. He had become such a good horse against the clock – a product of those indoor jumping outings – that I only had to look in a particular direction for him to turn. As I jumped the gate I looked to the right too quickly, and he tipped it with one of his hind feet. If he hadn't, he would have been third, not fourth, but I didn't really care.

We were picked to go to the World Championships at Luhmühlen on the strength of our efforts at Badminton and after we had won the Midland Bank Championships at Locko for the second year running. I was very excited to be picked, but my luck didn't last. After winning the Advanced section at Locko with P., I had had a crashing fall in the Novice with a young horse called Riotous. My confidence took something of a shaking, but I was determined to lay the jinx by riding him in another event the following week. It would 'be good for both of us', I argued. My mother didn't think that it was a very good idea at all. She could see that the very last thing I needed, just before Luhmühlen, was another fall, and an even bigger dent in my self esteem.

I didn't listen, I took Riotous to Rotherfield, and sure enough, we came another real purler. I was quite shattered.

Since the team was based at Wylye, in readiness for our departure to the World Championships, Lady Hugh suggested that we took Night Cap – who wasn't going to Luhmühlen – out for a school, to restore my confidence. It didn't work. In fact, I rode so badly that she actually had to shout to me to stop. Night Cap hadn't made a mistake, but Lady Hugh could see that I was making so many that poor old N. was having to work overtime to get me out of trouble.

'You'll have to go and get Priceless,' she said. So my mother went off down to the stables, collected P., brought him back, and I got on, feeling a complete nervous wreck. We jumped ten fences or so, and Priceless, obviously realising that there was a problem, decided to ignore the idiot on his back and take over – something that N. would never dream of doing! He jumped so well that my confidence in him, at least, was given a much needed boost.

Even so, I didn't particularly enjoy Luhmühlen. At Horsens I had been anxious, but confident, to an extent, in my own abilities. This time I was still nervous – but also very unsure of myself. My team mates: Lucinda, Richard Meade and Rachel Bayliss, sensing my troubles, were a tremendous help, but P. was best of all.

Again, we were picked to go first for the team. P. proved what a friend he was by jumping a clear if

Above: Success in a championship requires teamwork, and here Wol and I discuss my round in detail. My accuracy in relaying how the fences rode would be all-important for the rest of our team. Right: Dot, sensing my relief and excitement after the cross-country, puts a comforting arm around my shoulders. Far right: P. confidently tackling the seventh and final element of the water complex at the World Championships.

cautious round, with precious little help from me, collecting nothing but a few time faults. Had I not had those two setbacks with Riotous I would probably have come home with a faster time. However, the team won the gold medal, the great Lucinda won the individual gold, and P. was seventh, so we were very happy to have done so well.

That December I left Priceless at home, getting fat and woolly in the field, and went to the International Show Jumping Championships at Olympia. I returned to find that he was seriously ill. To start with it had seemed to be an attack of colic, but it had got worse and worse. Our vet from Devon, Don Attenburrow, came to see him and diagnosed leptospirosis, a rare disease caused by rats.

For five weeks after that we were up every night in shifts, monitoring P.'s respiration, temperature, and heart rate at regular intervals so that we could report his progress to Don. Poor little P. didn't know what had hit him. He was uncomfortable, listless and always lying down, a significant sign that he was not at all well. Like a human in a fever, he'd be sometimes hot, sometimes cold, so we were constantly changing his blankets. The slightest exertion was too much for him. At one stage we thought of taking him to Don's yard where he would have constant expert attention, but simply loading him

Don Attenburrow
Veterinary surgeon to the Holgate yard

Priceless is a prima donna, like a lot of great performers, so he is not particularly easy to deal with – unlike Night Cap who's as soft as a bun. I can't say I'm the only vet P. *likes,* because I don't think he likes any vet, but at least he tolerates me because we've been through a lot together. When he contracted leptospirosis – the only case I've ever known – he was a very sick horse indeed.

He was rocking, as he stood in his box, and was so jaundiced that his mucus membranes were as yellow as a lemon. We had him on intravenous drips and antibiotics for six weeks and during that time he was quite easy to do things with – a very obvious sign that he was ill! I went up to see him at least twice a week and spoke to the Holgates on the phone every day to keep a check on his progress. He was lucky to have such skilled nurses, but he was also a great soldier. We knew he was getting better when he started to be cheeky in the stable again!

The first inkling that something was wrong; Elaine's notes in P.'s daily diary.

The handwritten diary reads:

17 Friday
1982

P. has suspect colic.
blowing, high pulse,
wouldn't eat.
Hard droppings.
Drenched

P. didn't go in avenue

into the horsebox caused him such distress that we put him straight back in his stable again.

During those weeks I honestly thought we would lose him, and hardly considered the future at all. My only concern was that he should get better. I couldn't even begin to think whether he would ever regain his old form, and at the same time my morale was sinking fast. We had at last seemed to be getting somewhere. Now the bottom had dropped out of my little world.

It was three months before P. fully recovered, and he missed the whole of the spring season of 1983. While he stayed at home, getting fit again, I took Night Cap to the European Championships at Frauenfeld. I came home thoroughly depressed. There had been a difficult water fence which had caused a lot of falls because of people going too fast. As fourth member of the team, I was told to approach it very slowly – but I went so slowly that Night Cap stopped altogether. My mistake cost the team their title and convinced me that I was really not a very good rider at all and certainly not worthy of my good horses.

Despite being thrilled that Priceless was fit again, and all set for Burghley, I didn't particularly want to go because I was concerned that I'd let him down. My diffidence continued at the event. The night before the dressage, I was crossing the car park with a friend, Louise Bates, and pondering on the day to come. 'What's the matter?' asked Louise, and I burst into tears. I was utterly convinced that I didn't deserve to ride P. But the next day my fears were proved groundless. He did a very good dressage test and kept his lead all the way through the competition.

On the cross-country course that year my main problem was how to tackle the Brandy Glass fence. It had three elements: two sets of rails followed by a corner, all at slightly different angles, so that the quick route required a line through the eye of a needle. The difficulty lay in preventing the horse from squaring up to any one of those elements. Unless they were all jumped at a slight angle he would be bound to miss the last corner.

Had I not had problems at Frauenfeld, I wouldn't have hesitated to choose that fast route. P. was unwavering on any course that I set him, and completely reliable. It was also very much quicker, and could save us some time faults. However, in my current jittery, anxious state I found it very difficult to decide what to do.

Knowing about my dilemma, Malcolm Wallace proposed a solution as I stood in the ten-minute halt box, waiting to begin the cross-country, and *still* not sure which route to take! He'd been timing horses around the course all day and explained that if I arrived at the Flight Butts, the fence before the Brandy Glass, on the eight minute mark, then I would have time to take a

37

P. demonstrates his immense scope by sailing over the massive parallel bars at Burghley.

different, slower and safer route.

I set off, and sure enough, when I reached the bull-finch fence which Malcolm had mentioned, I looked at my watch and found that I was dead on time. Malcolm and Louise, who were following my round on the monitor, actually saw me lift my wrist to check the time, and apparently said: 'Right, she's okay now. She knows she's got enough time in hand to take the slow route.' The next thing they knew was that we were haring towards the quick one. And Priceless jumped it beautifully. I think jumping that one fence meant more to me than winning the whole event. The fact that I had enough confidence in him to trust that he would stay on such a difficult line, coupled with the verve with which he jumped it, gave me the most incredible sense of elation.

Of course when he won the entire competition, next day, it was thrilling. It's surprising what the Good Lord does for you. One minute you're literally grovelling on the ground and, the next, something incredible happens just to show that it's not really the end of the world. After all, nothing is simply handed to you on a plate. You get out of life what you put into it and things *will* go wrong. One has to deal with defeat as well as success, and I'm still learning.

The following year, 1984, was the year of the Los

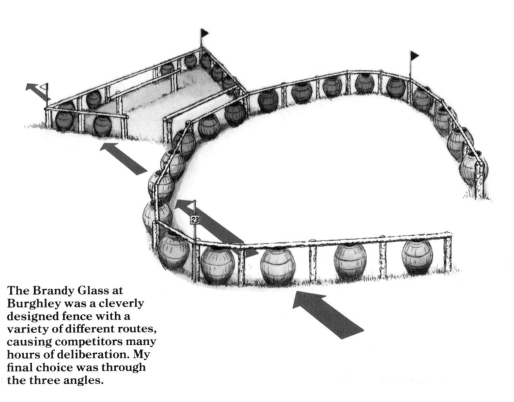

The Brandy Glass at Burghley was a cleverly designed fence with a variety of different routes, causing competitors many hours of deliberation. My final choice was through the three angles.

Angeles Olympics. P. and I were put on the long-list for the team, and exempted from Badminton. I had never imagined that I could aspire to an Olympic competition, but with my restored confidence and faith in P. I was determined to improve us both as much as possible, to do our team justice. To this end I made sure that we competed in enough One-Day Events in the spring to keep on the ball for the final trials. All went well, and we were selected to go.

About that time, Claire Henchy, an Australian friend of ours who is a very experienced event rider came to visit us for a few days and was co-opted on to our team. We asked her if she'd like to take charge of Priceless at the Games, and in the end she stayed with us for about four months.

When the horses set off for Los Angeles, Claire travelled in the 'plane with them. I knew I could trust her, as she is very capable and was familiar with P. and knew his little ways. I just had to keep my fingers crossed that they would have a good journey.

The riders flew out separately, but the minute we arrived we rushed to the stables. Night Cap, who had also travelled out as a reserve, had a little bit of a temperature – not out of the ordinary after such a strenuous journey. But Priceless, in his normal way, was in great form and raring to go!

The British horses arrive at Los Angeles airport. It is quite remarkable how adaptable horses can be. Priceless and Night Cap apparently enjoyed their first flight and caused Claire no problems.

P. and I relax in the sunshine at Santa Anita in the early days before the competition began.

We had about a week before the first phase of the competition, and spent the time making sure that the horses recovered well and adjusted to the climate. We used to get up at 5 o'clock each morning – which I hated – in order to have them exercised and back in their stables by 8, before the heat got too intense. At this stage, we didn't do a great deal of work, just gentle walking and trotting for a couple of days, then gradually more, when we were sure that they were completely rested. I remembered Richard Meade telling me a long time ago that it is important not to over-jump your horses in the few days before a big event. It is all too easy to make a mistake that could damage confidence, if nothing else. Priceless, who is not amused by jumping practice anyway, would, I'm sure, have agreed whole-heartedly with Richard! So, in the week leading up to the most testing event in the world we did hardly any jumping at all.

It was relentlessly hot – and that, plus the tensions of an Olympic event, made us all rather edgy. I was asked what position I would like to take in the team, and I didn't know quite what to say. Lucinda nobly volunteered to go first, but that seemed patently ridiculous: she was, after all, the reigning World Champion. I thought it was crazy for her to go in any position except last. Of all of us, she should be the one with the most chance of redeeming the team if our fortunes were failing, or going for Gold if all went well.

Team strategy always dictates that the most reliable people should go first and last, with the two less experienced in the middle. So that's what happened and I went first again. My favourite spot! Fortunately, I had quite a good draw, eighth, so at least I wasn't first to go or anything ghastly, as I'd been at Horsens.

On the morning of P.'s dressage I took him out for an early morning hack, then had a shower again before climbing into my dressage kit, as it was already uncomfortably hot. I put on my false bun, top hat and tails and Claire produced P., looking wonderfully smart, with his plaits, oiled hooves, and quarter mark squares on his bottom.

When it came to doing his test, he was a little on the keen side. Ten days at Santa Anita racecourse with nothing much to do and nowhere to go for a really good hack, had made him very fresh. He did a good test on the whole, but broke in one of his half passes to the right which was a shame, though fortunately it didn't make any difference to the placings at the end of the day.

After the dressage phase we moved down to San Diego for the cross-country. The course was very big, but seemed fair. There weren't any nasty traps for the horses, but I thought that the riders could very easily make mistakes. It was also very hot, which was an added worry.

We did everything possible to keep the horses happy – here Claire adjusts P.'s fly veil shortly after our arrival at San Diego, the cross-country site.

During the obligatory ten minute halt before the cross-country, Priceless cools down and recovers with the help of large electric fans and ice-packs on his poll.

Claire and I take Night Cap and Priceless for a good gallop on the excellent turf at Santa Anita racecourse.

At the Olympics

Claire Henchy
Priceless's groom at the Olympics

Really it was luck which played a big part in my being at the Holgates' yard in March 1984. I had been on holiday in South Africa for a few months and had had difficulty in extending my visa, so I arrived in the UK slightly earlier than planned. Having stayed with the Holgates before, it was easy for me to fit in with the team, and after my months of leisure it was great to be working with horses again. I was surprised and thrilled when they asked if I would stay on, perhaps to go to the Olympics as Ginny's groom. I jumped at the chance, and spent the next few months preparing under Dot's invaluable guidance.

There was a great deal of planning and preparation to be done before the Olympic team even set off for L.A. Priceless and Night Cap were placed in my care so that we could get to know each other, and I could become fully conversant with their normal condition, diet, work routines and equipment for every occasion. Only then would I be able to care for them in every eventuality and notice immediately if something was amiss.

The fitter P. became, the more intolerant and difficult to handle he was! To make matters worse, he was on a strict diet, which he hated. Whereas N. is a real gentleman in most respects, Mr P. is a character; very much the boss of the outfit, he is rather like a celebrity who doesn't for one minute allow you to forget his presence. He's pushy and *very* demanding. He could be horrible to groom, and would always manage to stand on my foot at least once, with a slight sideways step, timed so accurately that he rarely missed. Despite that, there's something about him which makes him everybody's favourite – I think it's because he *is* such an individual and perhaps just too smart at times!

The pre-Games preparations went well, and when the time came for us to leave for L.A. both the horses travelled comfortably on the 'plane, which had been one of our main concerns. Once out of quarantine and into their stables, they soon settled. It was pretty hot and sticky but each horse had a large electric fan by his box, which helped to keep them cool.

Santa Anita racecourse had hundreds of stables and lovely grass gallops, as well as dressage and jumping arenas, all carefully timetabled for use by the different countries. The atmosphere on dressage day was intense. Priceless, who knows when he is being plaited for a competition, stood like a rock so I was able to do heaps of tiny neat plaits in honour of the occasion.

The crowds were tremendous. I'd never before experienced the sort of power an audience can generate and sometimes it must have been hard for the riders to concentrate and not be completely overcome by the situation.

Once the dressage was over, things relaxed a little and we set off for the cross-country phase at Fairbanks Ranch. We had hoped it would cooler there, since it was near the coast, but the weather was still stifling. The course was beautifully built and very big, and the going was pretty firm. Tension mounted as our final preparations were checked and re-checked. For myself, just being there was awesome; I couldn't imagine what it must be like for a competitor.

Priceless stood patiently as I bandaged him – which seemed to take forever as the heat made the Vetwrap sticky and difficult to sew – but he became more aggressive once the weigh-in was complete. Fitting the weight cloth and saddle was crucial, but P. had other things on his mind at this stage and needed a person on either side of him whilst Dot girthed him up.

We drove to the beginning of the steeplechase to watch P. and Ginny tackle the big course with ease. He looked super and we were so thrilled with his fitness in that heat that Dot, Heather and I were quite a cheerful trio as we set off for the ten-minute box.

Two minutes ahead of time, they came in at a good sound trot. Once Ginny was off and away to have a drink and a talk with the Chef d'Equipe, we set to work. Heather faced P. into the fan whilst I sponged him down lightly and washed his mouth, face and dock. We checked his breathing rate, which was pretty good, double checked bandages, studs and shoes, dried off his reins and then applied protective Vaseline to his legs before I walked him round. At the two minute call Ginny mounted and rode to the start box. Again P. was very hard to control from the ground as our Chef d'Equipe led them into the start box. P. was raring to go: he put his best foot forward and rose to every challenge. I've never been so relieved and delighted as I was to see them both come home safe – and clear – at the end of the course. P. was tired and blowing hard but once I'd washed him down and walked him round he was soon relaxed and breathing normally again.

Next morning, I plaited him up for the vet check and he came out looking on top of the world – needless to say, he passed with no trouble and we set off back to Santa Anita for the final show jumping phase.

P. is a great little champion, resilient and talented in everything he does. He and Ginny were a formidable combination, but that, I know, was achieved solely through hard work, dedication and determination. I treasure the fact that I was able to make a small contribution to their partnership. The fact that they won silver and bronze medals made the experience even more special.

Below: Claire trots up P. for the panel of vets during the ten-minute halt. This is done for the benefit of the horse: any doubt about his fitness or soundness would have prevented him from continuing.

Right: Complete with jockey, the final girth checks are made.

On cross-country day we had to get up at half past five to drive to the course, as I was due to start at 8.20 a.m. Wol (Malcolm Wallace) and I, with Peter Scott Dunn, the vet, found ourselves stuck in an almighty traffic jam, with the clock ticking on, and for a while we wondered if we'd ever get there at all. I had visions of Priceless ready to start – without a rider. Eventually Wol was able to put his foot down, and with some inspired rally driving we got there in the nick of time.

Dot, Claire and my mother had everything under control, and P. was ready to go. As always, I put on his front bandages, with his tendon protectors and over-reach boots, and we set off for the start. The steeple-chase course was two circuits of a figure of eight, mind-bogglingly complex to follow, and I had already had nightmares about a repetition of the Hooge Mierde débâcle. Fortunately that wasn't to be, and P. zipped round despite the heat, making that phase seem easier than ever before. It was a still morning, which was unlucky for us, as there was no wind to ease the humidity, but our back-up team were ready at the ten-minute halt with electric fans, ice, and cool water.

As it was still early in the day, Malcolm Wallace could give me little information about the way the course was riding in those few precious minutes before I set off. I had to rely on our planned routes through the obstacles and hope that no unexpected complications would arise.

As it turned out, there were no problems – although P. took one stride at the water instead of two, which gave me an unnerving moment and caused the rest of our team to review their own routes through that fence. We finished just 0.4 seconds outside the time, and I was in seventh heaven. I galloped through the finish yahoo-ing and waving my arms in the air, completely forgetting all the rules about pulling up your horse in a calm and orderly fashion. I was so excited that Wol made me sit down in a chair and sip a can of Coke quietly, until he was sure I hadn't got a touch of sunstroke! P. had finished the course in great shape, and so did the rest of the team – we set off back to Santa Anita for the final

Waiting for the dressage is always a nail-biting experience.

P. and I begin our Olympic dressage test.

show jumping phase in great spirits.

I think that Friday was the worst and the longest show jumping day I shall ever remember. I was under great pressure, because I knew that we had to jump clear to win the bronze medal, and the whole team were aware that if we were to win the silver or even, perhaps, the gold medal, we needed clear rounds. It was a very tense afternoon.

Peter Robeson and Ted Edgar, who were there with our show jumping team, came to help us warm up over the practice fences. Peter put up a parallel for me and instructed me to hack into it without giving Priceless too much help. I'd only jumped about six fences when he shouted: 'Stop. Don't even attempt to jump another fence. That horse is trying his heart out.' Priceless was ballooning over them and doing everything possible to jump well. He just knew that it was important.

Perhaps the huge crowds around the arena warned him that something very special was about to happen; certainly I have never before sensed such an atmosphere on a show jumping day. At last we rode into the ring and I tried to remember everything I'd learned over the years: keeping P. balanced with his hocks underneath him, riding each corner, seeing a good stride into each obstacle, and trying not to think of the relief I would feel at the end of the round. P. jumped clear, so he won his individual bronze, and our team took the silver.

On the rostrum *everyone* burst into tears, and no one was ashamed of it. It was, after all, the Olympic Games. I personally that felt the two medals around my neck really belonged to a whole load of people: everyone in fact who had helped us to reach Los Angeles. But most of all those medals were P.'s.

Spectacular fireworks at the closing ceremony marked the end of the Olympics, but P. and I arrived home to Ivyleaze to find another party awaiting us. The village had clubbed together to present us with a little bronze to mark the occasion – and a huge sack of carrots! We had another big party – where P., the celebrity, became slightly bored after a while. Then he was spoilt to death for a few weeks as we let him down gently before turning him out for an autumn holiday.

The British Olympic Silver Medallists make the most of their glorious moment in the immense arena.

Below: I've always thought Priceless had a look of Arkle about him. Here photographer Kit Houghton did his best to show the hidden resemblance!

Right: P. and me taking our daily constitutional at Santa Anita racecourse, during the early part of our stay.

Dressage. Not a particularly flattering shot of either horse or rider. I look ready to burst into tears and P. doesn't seem very interested in the performance. The end result was more pleasing however, even though we both lost several hundredweight during those ten short, hot minutes!

Inset: A touching moment for my hard working mother and myself.

Cross-country. Having safely negotiated the very large upright fence into water we both sigh with relief and feel happy to attack the next obstacle: particularly P., who seems to be thoroughly enjoying himself.

Show jumping. A typical example of P.'s utter exuberance. His tail is almost vertical – one of his characteristics.

Overleaf: The ears back show total concentration. There is no doubt in my mind that P. knew the importance of this occasion; that kind of sense and will to please simply cannot be trained into a horse. The inset picture explains itself!

START

All in a day's work. P. opens the new British National Life building in
his own inimitable way, under the eye of Managing Director Roger Davies.

Don Attenburrow
Veterinary surgeon

The extraordinary thing about Priceless is that he's done all there is to do in the world of eventing and has survived with completely undamaged legs. Like that other great horse, Red Rum, he has the intelligence and courage to look after himself whilst performing to the maximum of his ability. Ironically his worst injury was the result of a kick in the field. His leg, when I saw it a few days later, was swollen and painful but didn't seem particularly serious. Luckily, I x-rayed it and discovered a hairline fracture. P. wasn't even lame but we were obviously concerned that the fracture might extend, so I suggested that he should be box-rested. By means of scintigraphy, a method of bone scanning which is still very rarely used, I was able to confirm the fracture, and chart its healing process. The great question was whether or not Priceless would be fit to run at Badminton, but thanks to this bone scan system I was able to say, eight weeks before the event, that the damage was completely resolved – and he went on to win. He is indeed a priceless horse.

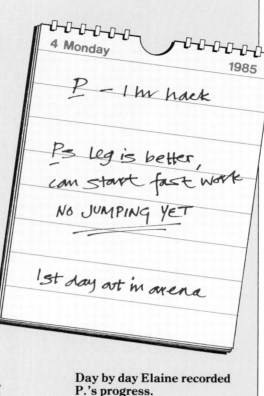

4 Monday   1985

P – 1 hr hack

P's leg is better,
can start fast work
NO JUMPING YET

1st day out in arena

Day by day Elaine recorded P.'s progress.

While P. was enjoying his new life of leisure in the field, Night Cap and I set off for Burghley. One evening, when I 'phoned the girls to check that everything was okay, they told me that P. had come in that night with a little lump on one leg. A kick, everyone thought. There was nothing I could do until I got home, but even when I did, and had a look at it, it didn't appear terribly serious. It was a small bump on the inside of a foreleg between the knee and the elbow. Though it was a little sore to the touch, P. wasn't even unlevel, let alone lame.

A few weeks later we took him to the Horse of the Year Show for a celebrity jumping competition. The fences on the actual course were quite small, but we put some larger practice jumps up first in the collecting ring. I could tell immediately that P. was unhappy about jumping them. This was most unlike him, and though he jumped the course without any trouble, I was sure that there must have been a reason for his lack of exuberance. There was no obvious explanation, but when Don came on a routine visit the following week, we asked him to

Twinkle-toes: all four feet off the ground at Badminton 1985. P. marks the spot!

The Footbridge at Badminton posed two main problems. Due to the width of the ditch, the spread was quite considerable, whilst the angle of the bridge itself increased its difficulty. Straightness is all-important at this type of obstacle. Any deviation to one side or the other would add unnecessary width to an already formidable spread. But P. has enormous scope and in this picture he really looks as though he's flying.

have a look at P.'s leg. He x-rayed the lump and discovered a hairline fracture on the bone. It could have snapped at any time.

I thought that this must be the end of P.'s career. Don, on the other hand, was reasonably hopeful. He has a machine which enables him to monitor the natural mending process of bone, so he could give us very precise instructions about what P. could and what he couldn't do. We had to keep him as still as possible, so he was stabled for the whole time. He could be walked out in hand for some grass each day but must be kept quiet and not allowed to lark around. Thanks to modern technology, Don could tell us exactly when it was safe to start light exercise, and though P. was stable-bound for three months it eventually paid off: the day came when the machine registered that the leg was completely sound again.

Don, who lives in Devon, is a long way from us, but without such inspired and assiduous care we couldn't

have achieved half the things that we have done. He has really saved P.'s life twice.

In spring 1985 P. won Brigstock, and with fresh hope we took him to Badminton – quite an achievement after the months of uncertainty the previous autumn. Badminton is a very special competition to win – the Wimbledon of the eventing world – and for me, as a local rider, it's an especially important event. I had always wanted to win it, if only to be able to look the neighbours in the eye. They have supported me faithfully through the years, but having not, yet, won our local competition, I felt that I had never quite lived up to their expectations.

On this occasion, P. gave me the ride of my life. It was the first time I had ridden two horses at such a big event and I had been rather unsure about my ability to cope, but Night Cap, who went first, gave me a confidence-boosting ride which put me in the best possible mood to attack the course again on P. We set off at a

great pace and never once needed to take a pull the whole way round. P. galloped and jumped with such style and assurance that I didn't need to upset his rhythm once.

It was not an easy course that year, and included not one but two bounce fences, which I always dread. To make matters worse, one of the fences at the Lake was a bounce into water, which I'd never tried before. I didn't know how on earth to ride it, but on my first trip round Night Cap jumped it beautifully, so at least when I approached it again on P. I knew it could be done! Priceless is a very good 'bouncer' and doesn't share my misgivings about them. I knew that as long as I brought him in at vaguely the right speed and on a good line he'd stay on it. Unlike N., he steadies himself automatically coming into a fence, so I just had to remember to ride him into it a bit more strongly than in my previous round – and it worked.

At the end of the course there were two corners with one stride in between. With most horses I would have needed to hook up and steady to make our approach as accurate as possible. Even then it would have been a tricky obstacle to negotiate fluently. But there didn't seem any reason to slow down. I saw a stride from quite a long way back, and P. was so straight and honest on his line that I could afford to keep the momentum and trust him totally. We finished that round with the fastest time of the day. As Badminton is one of the most difficult courses in the world, P.'s performance was quite incredible. I don't expect I shall ever experience another ride like that again.

Night Cap had gone clear as well, so they were lying third and fourth on the last day. It was more than I could have wished for, and when they both went clear in the show jumping, I was over the moon. I wasn't even watching the last two riders, who were lying first and second; I was busy patting the horses and yakking to everybody and saying things like: 'Oh isn't it wonderful',

Meeting the Queen was one of the proudest
moments of my life, only marred by a nagging
worry about P.'s penchant for nibbling. He
behaved impeccably, however, and didn't
even threaten to test his teeth on the coveted
Whitbread Trophy!

and 'It's all over, thank goodness!' The next thing I
knew was that somebody had had a fence down –
Torrance, who'd been in second place. That made
Priceless second and N. third, when Mark Todd went
into the ring.

Again, I wasn't particularly watching or listening,
because Toddy had jumped a clear round in Los Angeles,
and there was no reason at all why he shouldn't jump a
clear round that day, too. I heard an almighty scream
from the audience and turned to Dot saying: 'He's won.
Toddy's won', and gave her a hug, thinking: 'Well, at
least it's all over now.' Then Hamish, my fiancé, ran up
and said: 'You've won!' and I said: 'Don't be silly!
Toddy's won.' But he hadn't. He'd had a fence down. I
could not believe it. I burst into tears, I think Dorothy
burst into tears, too. In fact we all got very emotional
about it.

I always feel sorry for somebody who loses the lead
position because of a fence down in the show jumping,
but that day I felt in my heart that P. really deserved to
win. After all, Toddy had won the gold medal in the

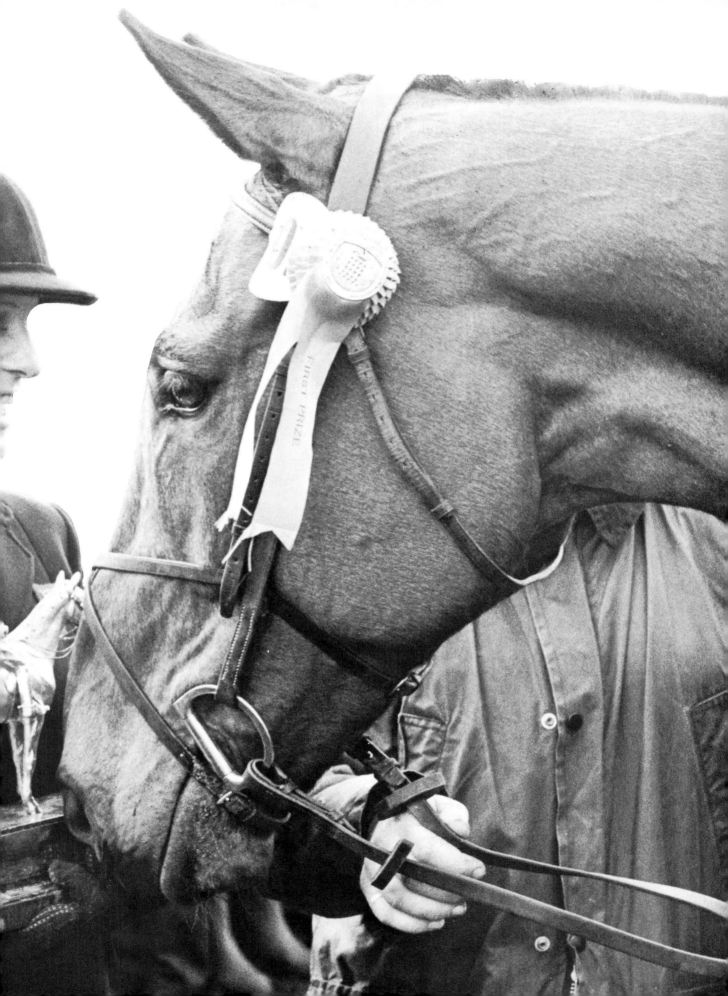

FIRST PRIZE

Games. Now this could be P.'s day. Nobody but the team selection committee had known about the problems we'd had with his leg. I'd told them that we hoped he could prove he was completely fit again, and he *had* done – in the best possible way.

That autumn the European Championships were to be held at Burghley, and the summer passed quickly as all our efforts were directed into preparations for it. The final team trial was at Locko, where dear N. at last beat Priceless into second place, giving N. a bit of a lift.

At Burghley Priceless was chosen to go fourth in the team, for the first time in our career. The fourth member is supposed to be able to pull up the team by doing a good round if the others have gone badly. Alternatively if the rest of the team have done very well, the fourth rider might be given the order to go for the individual title.

Burghley has always been my favourite event. Perhaps I prefer it because I've done quite well there over the years, but I always find the course more inviting than most. On this occasion though it was rather different. As the setting for the European Championships it was very big and, I thought, very difficult.

As a result of frequent visits to Jeremy Tree's all-weather gallops, P. was extremely fit – so much so that he got very steamed up as I rode him in for the dressage. Consequently I got steamed up, too, and it took the combined strength of mind of Dot and Pat Manning to stop me from panicking as I put on my hat and tails before entering the arena. Typically, P. produced one of his best tests ever, which stood us in very good stead in the team placing at the beginning of the cross-country.

Next day, as I circled round before the start of Phase D I felt rather flummoxed. Lord Patrick Beresford, our Chef d'Equipe, had just told me to 'go for Gold'. It was the first time I'd received that instruction in the whole of my life. Lorna Clarke and Myross had whizzed round with a confident clear, and my other team mates, Lucinda Green and Ian Stark, had also acquitted themselves well earlier in the day, putting our team in a very strong position. The stage was P.'s and mine, and it was rather a shock to my system. Lucinda came over to me and held up both fists, clenched: 'You can do it!' she said, and in that moment I suddenly thought: 'Well, yes, why not.' I gritted my teeth and off we went.

Two fences in particular were causing a lot of trouble that day. Fence 4, the Bullfinch, had worried me when I walked the course. It was a brush behind a ditch, rather like an open ditch on a steeplechase course. It had a bullfinch top to it for the horses to jump through rather than over, which made it very big. The only approach

Night Cap's turn to steal the show. Having beaten Priceless into second place at Locko, he leads the way into the arena to collect his Open Championship trophy.

Up, over and down! P. pays
close attention at
Burghley's Trout Hatchery
as he negotiates the log
into the water.

Left: Study in combined concentration during those long minutes in the show jumping arena.

As usual, Priceless has the last laugh.

P., myself and Winston, the British team mascot.

was downhill, but also at an angle, as there was a tree in the way which obviously made the fence wider and even more difficult. I hadn't seen many horses jumping it well all day, and I was a bit nervous about it. But P. jumped it spectacularly.

Towards the end of the course came the Maltings Wall: a rail, then four strides to a very acute corner, which had cause to be a real problem. However, it was just P.'s sort of fence, technically difficult and needing a horse who is accurate and straight. He jumped it quite beautifully and made it look fairly insignificant.

We went for all the quick routes on that course, and it was a thrilling ride. It wasn't as easy as Badminton, where we'd galloped so easily on the top of the ground, as Burghley has lots of ups and downs and twists and turns. But P.'s jumping was perfection. At the end of the day he was the only horse without time faults, and that was the most thrilling part of it. After all our struggling it seemed to us quite marvellous that P. was the only horse inside the time.

At the end of the competition our team won the European title and, though I felt happy enough already,

P. and I took the individual gold. The huge party that night overflowed from the Rémy Martin marquee into the stable area, so I slipped off to talk to P. In his usual fashion he stuck his ears back and tried to take a chunk out of me before capitulating and being friendly. I raised my glass to him and said: 'P. you're an absolute star!'

When 1986 came I felt that we'd had a pretty good innings. However, there was one more target. It was the year of the World Championships, to be held at Gawler, South Australia. I had very mixed feelings about it. I wasn't at all sure that I wanted to subject P. to such a long and rigorous journey after all that he'd done for me over the years. My mother and I, along with Don Attenburrow and Peter Scott Dunn the official team vet, discussed the pro's and con's endlessly until we were sure that we would be able to do everything possible to make the trip an acceptable one. Satisfied that P. would have the best care possible, I got down to our preparations.

As we were shortlisted for Gawler, we were excused Badminton and, instead, went to Wylye for the team preparations. We stayed there for four weeks – which

The victorious European Championship team parade at the Horse of the Year Show, 1985, where P., as individual European Champion, had his own lap of honour.

Dot, tutor and supervisor of operations, sometimes has to act as nanny as well! Here she makes sure P. keeps warm at Aldon, our one and only outing before settling into quarantine, Spring 1986.

was too long as far as P. was concerned, and he was a real pain in the neck. Previously he had only been to Wylye for dressage competitions, show jumping, or cross-country. He knew the system, he knew Lady Hugh's Mini-Moke, and he knew Lady Hugh herself, backwards! When he got there and realised he was stabled and appeared to be staying, I think he really did begin to wonder what on earth was going on.

In the meantime our team got to know each other better and synchronised our work programmes. For me it involved a daily drive of over an hour each way to work P. at Wylye. I also had to deal with N. who was at home preparing for Badminton, and I became thoroughly over-tired. P. meanwhile was getting bored. Since he had jumped pretty well all the fences at Wylye over the years, Lady Hugh had to go and find some new ones for him. We had great discussions about how we were going to keep him occupied, as she knows him as well as I do. Our fears were confirmed when he absolutely carted me round Aldon, a One-Day Event which was our only chance of a warm-up before the team horses

went into quarantine. P. realised straight away that this cross-country wasn't worth taking seriously. He jumped like a racehorse and I couldn't hold him at all. It was one of the most hair-raising rides I've ever had and wasn't even very fast, since I was trying to put on the hand-brake the whole way round the course.

P. went off to quarantine, and I, disgruntled, went home to have a serious think. It was imperative that I should be able to control him round a Championship course such as Gawler. A repetition of Aldon would spell certain disaster. Lady Hugh suggested that I should try a different bit, so for the first time in many years I swopped our Dr. Bristol for a slightly more severe roller snaffle. We took him out for a schooling session, and I found I was back in charge again – which was reassuring. He jumped very nicely. The problem was what kind of bit to use in Gawler. The Three-Day Championship course would be rather different from Aldon One-Day Event: the fences would be bigger, the distances greater and the climate more taxing, so P. might not require a stronger bit. After much heart-

Priceless didn't treat the Aldon course with a great deal of respect! It was an Open Intermediate rather than an Advanced competition, and it didn't take him long to realise that fact. Although here we are jumping the bank in unison, quite shortly afterwards it became apparent that we had very different ideas about the speed at which we should be going.

searching I took him cantering in his old Dr. Bristol, and decided to use it for our final trial at Wylye. He went very well, thank goodness, so I was happy.

P. always has to do something to himself before a big event. A week before his second Badminton he stood on a four inch nail, luckily without any major damage. Before Los Angeles he managed to catch his lip on a sharp edge and cut it open, about ¼-inch from where the bit lies, so that was handy as well! Before Gawler he banged his fetlock at the final trial, and was a bit sore for a couple of days. Fortunately, as on the other occasions, it didn't impair his performance – but it did add to our last-minute anxieties.

P. is a funny little horse. During his stay in Wylye he obviously wondered where all the competitions were. He was beginning to get fed up with the scene, and since the horses were all in quarantine, there were only certain areas we could ride in, which made it even more difficult to keep him fresh and happy. On reflection, we were lucky to have Wylye, because I'm sure that had he been anywhere else he would have gone quite nutty.

When the horses flew to Australia they went first to Torrens Island, for two weeks further quarantine. Priceless found that extremely boring, too, and became even more of a problem. It was difficult to know how much work to do and when to do it. I tried not to jump him too much because I knew he wouldn't appreciate it. In fact, I probably only jumped him twice in four weeks, and even that was to keep *me* happy, rather than him. I needed the practice even if Priceless didn't. I wanted to be sure of seeing my stride and getting the right pace.

The same applied to our dressage work. P. had to do enough to keep fit and supple, but he soon got bored and started to lean and to be awkward. The more I persisted the worse he would become. Although I was used to him by then it still made me panic; I felt we needed that dressage work, but I had to be very cool and cautious with him.

Although we did not do a lot of schooling, we worked P. hard on the gallops once the horses came out of quarantine and could be moved to their competition quarters at Roseworthy College. The Gawler course was steep and taxing and I was determined that P. should be fit enough to tackle it. At the same time I was concerned that I might be over-straining him by asking too much.

Ten days before the start of the Championships, another quite big One-Day Event was held in Australia. Some teams planned to compete in it, but we were dubious. Normally P. would have had at least three outings before a Championship, but ten days is not long, and a knock or cut at that first event could have spelled the end of Gawler for us. Eventually I decided

I wasn't just having a paddle! A great deal of careful deliberation went into the problems posed by the water jump at Gawler.

A thoughtful moment during the veterinary inspection.

64

This was one of P.'s best dressage performances. He really knuckled down to hard work and unquestioning attentiveness. There were times when he seemed to float along, using himself in the correct way to produce a smooth and pleasant test. He had always found dressage quite difficult because of the length of his back, but sometimes he would really produce a little bit of magic.

One of the most precious moments in our lives together. Not only had P. won Badminton, a feat in itself, but it was also a little dream come true.

Priceless demonstrates one of his little tricks: his ability to take off with his front legs and to clear the obstacle while still holding his hind legs on the take-off side for security!

Ears pricked, P. 'susses out' the problem within seconds, while I sit behind him trying to stay balanced without interfering.

Lengthy 'tarting up' preparations, including nail varnish, before the veterinary inspection.

P. launches himself into the water. I try to stay back ready for the impact of the drop - as a security measure!

Safely landed, both horse and rider quickly prepare for the exit.

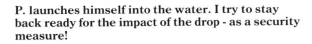

A moment of extreme happiness between friends. Elaine Pickworth, P.'s groom, Priceless and I all share our utter joy.

A shot of us both after negotiating the second water complex. I am somewhat behind the movement, but P., in his usual fashion, ignores my mistake.

After our near disaster on the first fence of the cross-country, we manage to regain our composure in time for Fence 2, where P. picks his feet up *very* carefully.

not to run him on the cross-country, but to just do the dressage and show jumping, *hors concours.*

After the event was over I took him round the first half dozen fences on the cross-country course to keep him happy and he jumped them very satisfactorily. In retrospect, I think I should have run him for the whole event as it would have taken care of his surplus energy. He was more pent up than I realised.

P.'s a smart boy. He'd done a lot of Championships, and he knew what was what. Once he arrived at Gawler and realised what all these preparations had been leading up to, he was quite beside himself with excitement – and he showed it! Before the dressage test began, he bucked – fortunately outside the arena; and he remained steamed up throughout his test. He didn't do as well as I knew he could, which was disappointing, but the team was still lying third at the start of the cross-country.

I hadn't honestly thought very much about the individual title. Obviously it had occurred to me that it would be wonderful to win it. I really felt that P. deserved to be World Champion and it would also be an ideal moment to retire him. But that was just a little fairytale thought that I pushed out of my mind as quickly as it entered.

Competition was fierce. Charisma had been going very well for New Zealand's Mark Todd, and Torrance Fleischmann's Finvarra was a strong contender from the USA, so I didn't think it was very likely that P. and I would win. Also, as we neared the event I became completely involved in our strategies for retaining the World team title. Really without thinking about it I found myself doing everything as part of a team, watching how other horses were going, walking the cross-country course together, following the same training system; which effectively removed all thoughts of the individual medal from my head.

Once P. had raced around the steeplechase and half of the roads and tracks, I had no doubt in my mind about his fitness, but I still wasn't in particularly good form as we stood in the ten-minute halt box, waiting to start Phase D. I had been chosen to go fourth again, so I had been able to watch earlier rounds on the close-circuit TV, and I admit it had made me pretty nervous. My orders were to go for a clear round rather than a fast time, and it was essential that we should do well to keep the team in the running.

Despite the roads and tracks and steeplechase phases,

Lord Patrick Beresford
Chef d'Equipe of the British team at Gawler

As first to go and pathfinder for our team Priceless had never once failed or feared or faltered. By the time I succeeded Malcolm Wallace as Chef d'Equipe he had matured into the best horse in England. With the unanimous consent of the rest of the team he had earned the right to the coveted number four position.

In the same way that many a good soldier will gladly undertake every form of training other than drill, Priceless was always enthusiastic for anything other than dressage. His test at Gawler was respectable rather than brilliant, but by the time he got into the starting box before the cross-country, his patience with the months of preparation, quarantine and general messing about had reached its limit. Off he charged, like a fighting bull into the ring, hurling himself at the first obstacle so impetuously that for a ghastly moment it looked as if Ginny might be unshipped. For my part, I felt totally sick. We had already had Clissy Strachan and Dazzle down in the water, and Ian Stark's Oxford Blue slipping up on the flat, so any mishap to Priceless would mean that we might as well have stayed at home. How could he get round if he behaved in this lunatic manner? I need not have worried: the further he went the more fluent he became, flinging the fences behind with

contemptuous disdain, finishing clear without a mark on him.

If Priceless had seemed rash before the cross-country, I have never seen him concentrate harder than he did on the final afternoon. At no moment was there the faintest likelihood that he would lower a pole, and he became World Champion with the same apparent ease as he had captured the European crown.

As Chef d'Equipe I will miss everything about him, from his amazing talent and consistency to the wonderfully level ring of his trot-up, crisp as a squad of marching guardsmen: but as a friend, which I am now proud to call myself, I can only rejoice that his long and faithful service has been rewarded by retirement whilst still at the very top of the tree.

P. still wasn't very settled when we set off. Physically he was fine, but mentally he was over the top. He was fed up with all the hanging about that he'd had to do over the previous weeks, and he wanted to get down to serious business again. As a result we nearly fell over the first fence. Fortunately that was enough to steady him, and by the time we reached the first real test, Fence 5, he was jumping brilliantly.

The fence which had caused our team the most heart-searching was the water complex – Dead Man's Pass. On first impressions we had decided to take the left hand route through it: a bounce on dry land into water, then two strides to a log, still in the water. The right-hand option was a rail, a stride, then another rail over a drop into the water, followed by a bounce over a log. We'd never bounced a fence in water before, neither had we seen it done, so we were very sceptical about that route.

Clissy, who went first for our team, followed our left-hand route and fell as she landed in the water. That made the rest of us wonder whether we'd have to change our minds. We watched a few more horses, and discovered that on the right-hand side they were actually fitting two strides instead of one between the first elements. This meant that they could angle as they landed in the water to fit in a tiny stride before jumping

On our way!

A long way from Exmoor. Diana Scott joins Dot to congratulate her hunter, the new World Champion.

the rail. It seemed totally against all jumping principles (we'd measured the distances very carefully), but that was the way it worked, and Lorna Clarke and Ian both rode it successfully. The New Zealander Tinks Pottinger jumped it correctly with the bounce, but later when Mark Todd tried to do the same, he fell. I decided to go for the angle to give myself a bit more room, and Priceless jumped it brilliantly, so I was lucky. Our team strategy had worked.

Further along the course came two very difficult corners which, it turned out, only two people attempted, Michael Plumb and myself. It was very risky, as the first corner was a right-hander followed by a left turn into a left-hander, so it actually encouraged the horse to run out. The second corner was big and at a very acute angle, but Priceless is so accurate that when I jumped the first and found he was still straight I thought: 'Right! We're on.' As I sent him towards the second element, my heart was in my mouth. Luckily we had a good stride, and he never faltered for a moment. But there are very few horses with whom I would have attempted to jump it.

At the end of the course I found that we hadn't done too badly. We'd got round and finished with 17 time faults which put us in second place individually. The team was lying second, too.

Home at last. Dot and P., above, disembark carefully after the flight.

After six long weeks Priceless, left, sets his feet once more on good ol' English soil — and greets my mother with a mouthful of Pommy grass.

Showing off his newly acquired rug at his celebration party, above right, P. ignores his guests and gets on with more important matters.

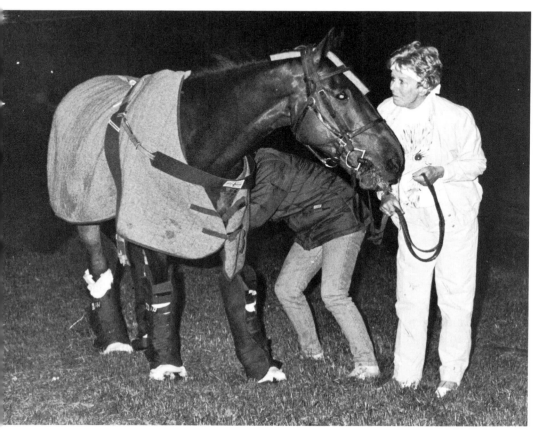

70

Tinks Pottinger was the clear leader, but at the last veterinary inspection before the show jumping, her horse, Volunteer, came out lame and was spun. P. jumped clear, and became the new World Champion.

It was very sad for Tinks, and I would far rather we had won it from the top, and not through someone else's misfortunes. Tinks had gone fast enough to be the only rider without time faults – but had suffered by hitting a fence which had lamed Volunteer. P., I think, was destined to win that event, he had given a lot during his career, and he was a true World Champion.

We returned from Gawler to a monumental reception in the village, followed by a garden party for P. and all the people who had helped us to win our medals. P. joined in, of course, and spent the afternoon eating grass, knocking over bottles, and behaving really badly. It was a great way to celebrate his success.

Thirteen isn't particularly old, but Priceless had done eight years solid Three-Day Eventing, and I doubt if there are many horses who have done so much in such a relatively short space of time. In order to stay at the top, horses have to maintain a very high standard of excellence, and he'd kept that up for three years. It is just not possible to stay at the top indefinitely, and I knew that there would come a time when he'd start to lose his edge.

As team policy is always to take young horses to the Olympics, and P. would be fifteen by the next Games, I knew that he would not be considered. I didn't see any point in trying to regain the European title and thus risk a terrible failure. Perhaps his dressage would deteriorate, either because he was older or because he was becoming too cunning. He already knew the test backwards. Maybe he would have a problem across country. Either way, I just could not have lived with myself if I had been greedy at his expense. I don't think there's another horse in the world who has *never* had a refusal across country, and I didn't want to spoil his record.

So I decided to retire him after Gawler. But first I wanted him to go and enjoy himself at a couple of One-Day Events. And he did, thoroughly! At Gatcombe he won the National Championship and was second overall in the British Open, behind the USA's Bruce Davidson. He would have won the Open if I hadn't made a mess of the cross-country and taken him the long route through a fence when we should have gone for the short option.

The following week we went to the Scottish Championships at Thirlestane Castle. He was a bit silly in his dressage test because he was irritated by flies – he's always been sensitive about them in the summertime – so he didn't get a very good mark. As I didn't want to go

Mixed emotions at the end of a great partnership. Happiness, sadness, but above all immense pride in my best friend, Priceless.

flat out on the cross-country, we finished tenth.

In a way, I saw in his fussiness about the flies a small sign that he had done enough. His concentration on the flat was not what it used to be. To maintain a high standard of finesse in dressage, horses have to be utterly concentrated and not at all big for their boots. Priceless is, and always has been, rather big for his boots!

Despite the rigours of the last few years, P. is still 100% sound. He's always been a careful jumper and he has probably got the best legs in the country. They're immaculate, without a single lump or bump to show for his experiences. It seemed like a good time to stop.

I chose the Horse of the Year Show as a suitable occasion on which to retire P., as I knew I was due to be awarded the Horse and Hound Trophy for Horseman of the Year. It would be a very special occasion for both of us, and we'd be in the ring alone, together. As my decision was announced to the audience, and Princess Michael of Kent presented me with the trophy, I burst into tears. I felt desperately proud of P. – and those moments in the spotlight were some of the most emotional of my whole life. I don't regret that decision for a moment.

So now P.'s job is hunting, where he started his career. Together we went out with the Beaufort during the autumn of 1986 and he loved every minute of it. Since then, my great friend Louise Bates has been hunting him in the Pytchley country, and she reports back weekly – to tell me how fantastic he is! It seems fitting that a horse who has given me so much joy can now give similar pleasure to a good friend. And P., of course, is having the time of his life . . .

Back where he started, Priceless and I out hunting with the Beaufort. He surprised me by behaving like a complete gentleman, and I was thrilled at the obvious delight with which he took to his new job.

Louise Bates
MFH Pytchley Hunt

Priceless is so human, it's unreal. He knows quite definitely who he is and what he has done, and it has made him a very confident chap. I've known him since he was five, so even before he came to my yard, I'd guessed that he would be a very proud horse to ride, and he certainly is. He makes me feel like a million dollars when I'm on his back. He adores hunting, and makes the day enjoyable no matter what the weather or the conditions are like.

Everyone treats him like a king and he is very spoilt. Priceless was accustomed to having a view of the yard so we changed our horses around to accommodate him and put up a special windbreak since he doesn't like having a grid across the top of his stable door.

Priceless is very particular; if we try to use a different type of brush to groom him he registers his disapproval by nipping his chest, his rugs, and anywhere else handy if

we're unlucky! And when he's had his playtime in the field we have to take out special horse nuts to catch him. If we offer him any others, that smell different, he just kicks out and runs away.

P. is already a very popular person in the district. One senior member of the Pytchley Hunt, Mr Bob Hemp, called to see him and take some snapshots as soon as he arrived here, because he's always admired him so much. He also brought a large sack of carrots which P. was very pleased about. He's a radio star now, as well as a T.V. one, as he's been interviewed on Radio Northampton.

With Priceless in my yard I think I must be the most fortunate person on any hunting field.

Louise is Master of the Pytchley, so P.'s 'retirement' is hardly an anti-climax after his eventing career. Instead he leads the field when they go out hunting, and Mr P., of course, thinks he's the bee's knees!

Behind the Scenes

The action packed days of an international event are the culmination of months of dedicated training and effort. My mother, who runs our yard at Ivyleaze; Dorothy Willis, our helper and adviser, and Elaine Pickworth, P.'s groom, have all played vitally important parts in Priceless's phenomenal career.

Out Hacking

Heather Holgate

Mr. P. is priceless, in every sense of the word, so hacking him out is never dull, although he may think otherwise. At the beginning of each year he would come in from his winter break, overweight, incredibly hairy, and looking more like a Highland steer than a horse. My job would be to help get him fit again with daily hacking. Secretly he'd be pleased to be back in work, but he would have hated to think that we realised! The first time I tacked him up to ride him I often used to wonder if I had the right girth. Certainly his name would be written on it in bold letters, but whereas before it had fitted quite snugly, now there would be a vast expanse of brown fur between the buckle and the saddle strap. Surely it can't all be fat, I would think, struggling vainly with frozen fingers to make the two ends meet. It wasn't, it was air, and when finally P. became bored with the game he would deflate quietly, his stomach would reduce to half its size, and I would find that I could do the girth up quite easily after all.

My humour wouldn't improve as P. slouched out of his stable. He has a wonderful trick of elongating his neck and holding his head horizontal so that his body is as far away from the person leading him as possible. I always like to insist that horses walk alongside me, shoulder to shoulder, and at some of P.'s early events, I would be so ashamed of his shuffle that I'd lead him round behind the horseboxes in case I bumped into someone I knew!

On his first day out and heading for the mounting block, P. would look almost enthusiastic for once and my hopes would be raised: perhaps this year things would be different. Not for long though, because once on his back and reaching down to do up his girth, I'd suddenly find myself propelled towards his ears. Quick as a flash, he would yank his head down and pull the reins out of my hands, leaving me looking a complete fool with the girth in one hand and no reins at all.

P. quite enjoyed his first hacks because they were a novel experience after his holiday. He'd look at the scenery with interest and wouldn't bat an eye at the traffic, unlike Night Cap who, in that first week, always has the vapours whenever a lorry approaches. That sort of thing is beneath P. although he will have an occasional buck, generally ensuring that he catches his rider again as they come back down to earth. I've never known him buck harder than he thinks his rider can handle. The only time he would be a little naughty was when, for some reason best known to himself, he would try to bite a horse I was leading from him, sending it off at a tangent and leaving me suspended in the air between the two of them. Fortunately it didn't often happen.

We always make sure that our horses walk out when we take them hacking, but P. would always drag his toes if he could possibly get away with it. He also had a trick which we called the '99 bonk' walk which he'd bring into play if he thought he'd done enough for that day. He would go slightly unlevel behind and the only thing we could do was take him home on a long rein, and wait until tomorrow!

I try very hard to vary our hacking, by planning different routes for the horses, and taking them off in the lorry to give them a change of scene. They all have their own favourite rides and sometimes if I think they're getting a bit stale we'll let *them* choose which way they want to go for a change!

P. always enjoyed going somewhere new and when we arrived and let the ramp down, he would heave a great sigh and stand at the top to have a good look to see where he was. He always entered into the spirit of those outings although he thought a lot of our local rides were rather boring. For some reason he always pre-ferred to turn right rather than left at the bottom of our drive, and to go on one particular ride through a little village called Alderton. I can't imagine what's so special about that route, except that it hasn't any hills so it involves less work!

We do plenty of walking, and occasionally slow trotting, up hills to get the horses fit. They puff and pant at first but P. always seemed to prefer a shorter bout of hill work to a longer hack, even though it required more effort. As he got fitter I had to be very careful about him shying. He'll shy at absolutely nothing, just when you're congratulating yourself on the fact that he *hasn't* shied at something that did look scary. His shy is like driving into the back of a car – the whiplash effect is quite dramatic – so his riders quickly learn the importance of staying alert. P.'s a great character and he's always one jump ahead!

In Training

Dorothy Willis

A really good event horse doesn't just need natural ability. He must really want to do all the things his rider asks of him. That's what made P. so amazing. He enjoyed his work and he loved to learn something new. The only problems we ever had were when he felt he'd done an exercise enough times already and got rather bored with it. He has an incredibly quick mind; there are some very good thinkers amongst the horses at Ivyleaze but none can quite equal him! As his mind is so active and he learnt things very quickly we had to work overtime to keep him occupied and to stay one jump ahead.

As Badminton, in April, is the first major event of the year we would bring P. in on the 4th or 5th of January to start work. It was harder to get him fit for a spring event than an autumn one, because during the winter he was roughed off in September or October and had a much longer break than the five or six weeks between

Even close friends could be forgiven for not recognising P. when he came in from his holidays in January. Woolly as a bear, and sporting a rather large tum, he certainly did not look like a potential World Champion.

Just three months later — and what a difference! Slimmed down, toned up and polished to perfection, P. looks every inch an aristocrat — and knows it.

the spring and autumn seasons. When he came in after Christmas he was less fit than at any other time of year, yet he was going to do the most difficult Three-Day Event in the world. Getting fit for Badminton was a race against time.

When P. was roughed off, he'd go out in the field for a complete rest, with plenty of hard feed and hay to help keep him warm since there's not much grass around at that time of year. On rations like that it's easy for horses to get a bit fat, and Priceless, who finds putting on weight the easiest thing in the world, would come in from the field looking like a bullock! That meant he had to work even harder, not only to build up muscle and get fitter, but also to regain his figure!

The only way to lose weight was by dieting and exercise. Like a lot of people, P. becomes very ratty if he's on a diet, and after the first couple of winters we realised it would be better all round if we could stop him getting fat in the first place – especially if he was to be slim again in time for Badminton. Along with weekly records of exactly what we gave him to eat, we'd also note down P.'s girth and stomach measurements. Year by year we could compare his progress in becoming fit, and could check that his feed and work were effective enough.

Straight from the field, we would hack him out for the first week or two, building up to two hours a day as he got fitter. After the hack he'd start by doing a mixture of dressage and jumping. As his schooling became more difficult and strenuous, the hacking would be cut down, so that in total he'd have about two hours work a day.

Each day, when he came in from his hack, Ginny would school him for about half an hour. I would usually be in the arena while they worked: not to teach Ginny as such (they were beyond that stage) but to discuss the way P. was going, in order to attain the degree of finesse that is the aim for an Advanced horse. I also lunged him regularly over poles, to help him become more collected and rounder. He didn't particularly like that, as it was rather hard work and I don't think he was very impressed with me as a result.

A lot of people said that Priceless would never be fast enough to get inside the time on the cross-country phase of a Three-Day Event. I wasn't sure, but I did know that as he became more confident and fitter, and as he had more practice at actual galloping as opposed to cantering, he seemed to be speeding up.

To start with, we did a lot of work to build up his muscles and to make him more engaged, with stronger hindquarters. Hill work helped, but cantering was the most important. When Ginny first moved to Ivyleaze we searched around until we found a farmer's field near by with a half-mile stretch along the side of the road.

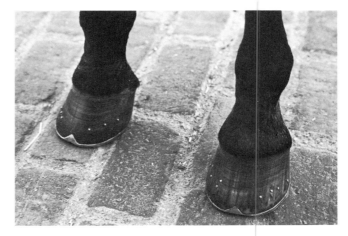

P.'s feet are as sound as they are safe.

Ginny would canter Priceless alongside the wall whilst I drove the car beside her. It wasn't exactly like another horse for P. to race against – we didn't want him to do that – but it helped to give Ginny an idea of the speed at which they were travelling and how fast they ought to be going. It gave them a bit more incentive than ploughing along on their own.

For cross-country schooling, Priceless always went to Wylye. It's a little difficult to ride an Advanced horse 'cold' over big fences, but they would usually go a couple of times before the start of the spring season to give both him and Ginny a bit of a whizz round, boost their confidence, and help them to get their eye in for the coming season.

Brian Higham

Brian Higham, Stud Groom to the Duke of Beaufort, always clipped Priceless before a big event. 'He had a hunter clip for eventing, leaving the saddle patch and his legs. I used to clip him before Burghley, and at the end of January for Badminton. In the summer before the Olympics we clipped him so that he would stay as cool as possible in the heat. He was a very intelligent horse and quite easy to handle, but I always knew that if I'd been a bit firm with him he'd have been doubly difficult next time.'

Feeding

Heather Holgate

For Priceless, as with all our other horses, we try to follow a feed programme which is as close as possible to a natural way of life. Horses are grazing animals, and it isn't natural for them to be stabled for hours without food, so we give them small quantities of grass and hay regularly to keep them happy.

P. enjoys his food so feeding him is rarely a problem! The only time I did have any difficulty was when he was sick with leptospirosis and had to be fed half a pound of glucose. I mixed it with water and put it in a huge plastic syringe – which P. pretended to think was terrifying – to insert in the side of his mouth. Of course he put his head in the air and glucose went everywhere. I was covered, P. was covered and it dried into a horrible white sticky mess. Fortunately we got enough down him to do some good!

Before we took P. to Gawler we also tried to ensure that he was accustomed to the kind of feed that he would be eating out there. Racehorses usually have six months off before they are expected to perform after a journey across the world, and it was asking an awful lot of P. to subject him to a stressful journey, place him in an unfamiliar environment, and then compete in a World

Championships in a matter of weeks.

To help him, I wanted to minimize the stress factor as much as possible, and one way I could do that was by ensuring that he got used to the food he would eat in Australia, while he was still in England. It was not an easy thing to do. By the time the authorities in Adelaide had decided the source from which they would supply the competitors' feed – and getting food from the same source was very important if my plan was to work – a ship which would have transported it to England free of charge had already left. This meant that we had to fly it over, which was very expensive.

Even that wasn't the end of the story. The main feedstuff – oaten straw – arrived in England, and P. nibbled a handful for a publicity photo to mark the occasion. That was all he *would* eat since the sample was so appalling that I don't think even cattle would have touched it, let alone P.! Eventually, just two weeks before we were due to fly out, a shipment of Australian meadow-hay arrived, which I could mix with the best of the oaten straw to feed with the sample of their oats; so P. was on Australian forage for at least a couple of weeks before departure. Spillers, who provide our horse nuts and event mix, sent their recipe over to Australia, so that at least the proportions would be the same. As a result, P.'s feed routine was changed as little as possible. No one can tell how much or little it affected his final result, but as he did settle into his new environment very well I think the effort was worthwhile.

Travelling

Dorothy Willis

Priceless has always travelled amazingly well. Even when he had to spend long periods of time in cramped conditions with horses he didn't know, he still would come out at the other end as if he'd actually enjoyed it.

Most horses are affected by long journeys. Night Cap is a nightmare because he is difficult to keep weight on at the best of times and will always worry some off if he has to spend any length of time on the lorry. P., by comparison, never loses weight.

He travelled to British competitions by lorry, and crossed on the ferry to the European events at Horsens, Hooge Mierde and Luhmühlen. Of course, some lorries are better ventilated than others, and it can make a huge difference if the driver is careful and considerate so that the horses aren't thrown around. Priceless really didn't know he was born, because for the most part he was driven around in a real Rolls-Royce of a lorry, thanks to our sponsors, British National Life.

Heather, also, is far more careful than most lorry drivers and, when crossing to Europe, she would go to enormous lengths and drive for hours to avoid a long or choppy sea passage.

To get to the Olympic Games and Gawler, P. had to fly. Los Angeles took 13-14 hours, but Australia was 40 – so long a journey that Heather insisted that we wouldn't let him go at all unless she or I could fly with him in the 'plane. The authorities agreed, and I went with him.

At the airport, when I arrived to take charge of P. he was very surprised. I was the person he associated with schooling and he obviously couldn't figure out how on earth he could be expected to work on Stansted airfield! But he soon realised that for this trip at least I was Elaine's 'stand-in', and his attitude to me changed completely. From then on, for the duration of the journey, he kept a very sharp lookout for me and the 'goodies' he'd learned to expect from Elaine.

In fact Priceless travelled a lot better than I did! I suppose I was slightly more anxious than he was, because I knew what was going to happen. Priceless, who's not a blob, guessed that something was in the offing, but unlike some horses who find unfamiliar situations upsetting, he simply settled down to take a keen interest in everything that was going on.

In the 'plane the horses travelled in stalls facing forwards. Going to the States, they were housed in threes, in stalls about six feet wide. For Australia, they went in twos and had the equivalent of a stall and a half each, as it was a much longer journey. P. had a few more feet to move left or right but he still wasn't able to lie or turn round.

Horses don't lie down to sleep very often and can rest just as well standing up, but a 'plane journey is still very tiring for them. P. had to use his back legs to brace and support himself, especially on take off and landing. As the 'plane goes up the floor slopes quite steeply, so he would be thrown right back on to his hocks, and again, on landing, he would have to work to stay upright.

We had four stops on the way to Gawler and six on the journey back, but Priceless coped very well with it all. We adjusted his feeds so that he was fairly hungry when he was loaded on to the 'plane and could be given something to eat just before take-off to distract him. I always put a bridle on him for take-offs and landings so that I had more control, and he paid more attention to me, but really he was very good and not in the least bit upset by it.

Once the horses reached their destination, they spent

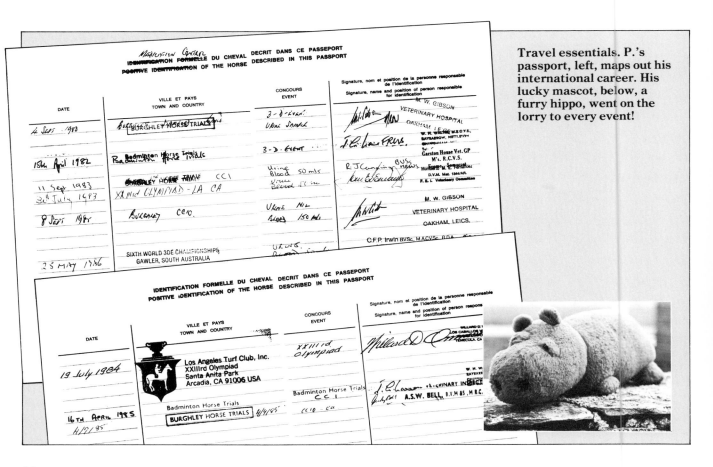

Travel essentials. P.'s passport, left, maps out his international career. His lucky mascot, below, a furry hippo, went on the lorry to every event!

In quarantine at Wylye, P.'s intelligence caused us considerable worries. Keeping him happy was just one of the problems, but, thanks to Lady Hugh, we managed to entertain him successfully up to the day of departure.

Aldon 1986. One of those days where things did not go quite according to plan. Priceless attacks the cross-country with vigour - and at very great speed. He ignored all my instructions to slow down and consequently gave me a very interesting ride!

P. found the veterinary
inspection a complete bore
and waste of time! Here he
shows his clear distaste
for the whole
performance.

An unusually relaxed
moment in our full
dressage kit!

'If' - the little word with the big meaning! Only a few more fences to go; *if* only....

The British World Champion team's lap of honour. All the riders and horses clearly show their joy.

Overleaf: Horse of the Year Show 1986. The most emotional moment of my life: the retirement of my brave and brilliant Priceless.

most of the following day lying down in their stables, recovering. Some were a bit colicky or off their food because they were so tired, but not P. Despite everything, he was still fairly fresh. We led him out in hand to stretch his legs and graze but had to be particularly careful to choose patches of long grass for him. The ground was quite sandy, and since P. is a real pig about eating grass he would have happily gulped down mouthfuls of sand, as well, in his haste!

Priceless at home

Elaine Pickworth

Travelling Checklist

Before every event, Elaine made out a list of all the tack and equipment Priceless would need, so that when the horsebox was loaded up she could be sure that nothing was forgotten. A typical list looked something like this:

- Work bridle, girth, numnah, boots and bandages
- Dressage saddle
- Jumping saddle
- Best bridle
- Reins for dressage, jumping and a spare set
- Nosebands – spare
- Bits – spare
- Show girths for dressage, jumping and a spare set
- Over girth
- Weight cloth and lead
- Breastplate with martingale attachments
- Martingale
- Best bandages
- Best boots
- Overreach boots
- Leg protectors
- Stable rugs
- Sponsor's best rugs
- Lunge cavesson, side reins, lunge rein and whip
- Grooming kit
- Plaiting box
- Veterinary box
- Spare shoes
- Stud box
- Buckets
- Feed manger
- Hay nets
- Feed
- Hay
- Scoops and measures
- Mucking out tools
- Fly veil and fly repellent
- Mane wrap (to keep P.'s mane flat and neat!)

When I first began working at Ivyleaze in 1984 it was January and the horses were just coming in to prepare for the spring event season. Each groom is allocated at least one horse who's in full competition work, so that we all have a chance to go to events. I was given Priceless, Night Cap, and a novice called Titch.

P. was always my favourite although it did take me a while to get used to him. He's a very individual horse, in the same way that some people are individuals because they have strong personalities, and he seemed quite ferocious at first. He can be naughty in the stable, particularly when he's fit, but he's cheeky rather than nasty; he might snap his teeth when he's being groomed or having his rug done up, but he's not trying to hurt you. If he nips you, by accident, he's terribly shocked and apologetic. I could always tell if he was feeling off colour because he wouldn't snap his teeth at me – it's a sign that something's wrong.

He's very different from Night Cap, who is a gentleman by nature and would hate to do anything wrong. P. tries to get away with as much as he can but he's such a character that he always manages to worm his way back into people's affection.

As it's important for horses to have a regular routine, P.'s life at Ivyleaze followed a very similar pattern from day to day:

6.30 am Morning feed
P.'s always hungry, so he was pleased to see me in the morning because he knew that it meant food.

8 am – 9.30 am Ride out
I rode P. quite often, but he was not very keen on hacking. He thought it was boring, and he didn't see why he should waste his energy on it. Whoever was riding him had to work overtime to make him walk out and keep up with the others. Sometimes, when he was plodding along at the back, it was easy to forget that you were riding a World Champion.

10 am Schooling
When he was preparing for an event, Ginny would usually school him for half an hour in the outdoor arena after he came back from his ride.

1 pm Lunchtime feed

P. puts on weight really easily, so quite often he has to go on a slimming diet. He still gets fed, along with the others, but he never thinks it's enough, so he hangs over his door, snapping his teeth like a crocodile, just to remind everyone that he's still there and hungry.

His stable is right next door to the feed room, and at one time we were quite worried that he'd end up with more muscles on one side of his neck than the other because of his habit of craning around the corner looking for food. His neck gets longer and longer as he stretches over the door, but from inside the feed room you can never see his eyes, just his nose, because that's as far as he can reach. If you actually touch his nose he's terribly embarrassed – it's as if he thinks we can't see him, just because he can't see us!

The other grooms and I only ever feed him at the regular times and he knows it; but he'll bang his door if Mrs Holgate or Ginny come into the yard, in the hope that they'll realise that he's absolutely starving and will take pity on him.

2 pm Turn out

All the horses are turned out for at least half an hour a day, so that they can roll and relax. P. wears boots in case he slips up or knocks himself, and usually a New Zealand rug, as well, if he's been clipped. He's very independent and he doesn't mind going out on his own, even though horses are herd animals and are supposed to prefer company. Quite often he'll go out with Night Cap because they're good friends and are usually ridden at the same time. They kick and play, and if there's any water around, P. will stand in it and paw with his foot so that Night Cap gets covered. He rolls a lot too – not just a quick roll, both sides and preferably mane and tail as well. If it's going to be done, it has to be done properly as far as P.'s concerned.

He can be very difficult to catch, especially if it's a nice day and he thinks he'd rather stay in the field and eat for a bit longer. I just have to stand in the field until he comes in, reluctantly digging his feet in at the verge by the gate in the hope that I'll change my mind and turn him out again. When I don't, he trails into the yard behind me at a snail's pace, snapping his teeth at my elbow.

When he and Night Cap are roughed off for a holiday they think that it's great fun at first, and concentrate on eating as much grass as possible. After a while, though, they get bored and start coming down to the fence to watch everyone schooling in the arena beside their field. Then they put on a bit of a show of their own and set off up the field with lots of fly bucks, just to upset the youngsters inside the school!

3.30 pm Strapping

When P. comes in from the field I strap him off. That's when he's most likely to have a bit of a snap, because he's very ticklish and he doesn't much like being groomed. His ears go flat back against his head and he gnashes his teeth and swishes his tail throughout the operation. His most sensitive spot is just behind his elbows and he hates me to brush there; if I try to get the mud off with my fingers he practically collapses in a heap; his whole body creases over because he's so ticklish. If he bites my coat I'll growl at him, but he'll already know he shouldn't have done it; he'll look at me as if to say: you shouldn't have got in the way!

Of course he knows exactly what he's doing, and he was much worse when I first started looking after him; he used to wind me around his little finger. I had to learn about his little tricks by trial and error; for instance, I can't tie him up with a quick release knot – he'll pull it

undone in a second – I've had to devise a different type which he can't undo.

Funnily enough he's very good about having his mane and tail pulled, and he actually *likes* being plaited because it means he must be going somewhere. To P., going out hunting – or, in the old days, to an event – is like going to a party.

5 pm Evening feed
After we've finished grooming, the horses are fed and then left alone for some peace and quiet, to relax.

9 pm Final check
Later in the evening I go out to check that P.'s all right; making sure that he's warm and has enough water. If he was in hard work, then he'd have another feed as well, which he was very pleased about.

... and away
Going to a competition, P. was really in his element. He was very alert, spooking at all sorts of silly things that normally wouldn't bother him, and even more of a devil to groom than usual.

When Ginny was riding him he would become very excited because he knew something was about to happen. At the beginning of a cross-country phase he'd fidget and buck, but the moment he'd finished and Ginny had got off he'd switch off again. I could walk him round and he'd relax immediately, as if nothing had happened at all. He's just very clever, he doesn't believe in wasting energy.

At home, after an event, it usually took him a few days to wind down. Then he relaxed back into his ordinary routine and slouched in and out of the field as normal; to look at him, nobody would believe that he could get over a two-feet pole!

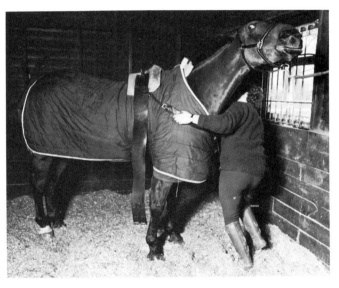

P.'s stable, left, ideally situated next to the feed room. When he was fit and on a slimming diet he would hang over the door, snapping his teeth and demanding food from whoever walked past.

Above. A ticklish moment. Priceless is not the easiest horse to groom or rug up, and puts on a tremendous show of ferocity. He would hate to hurt anyone, though!

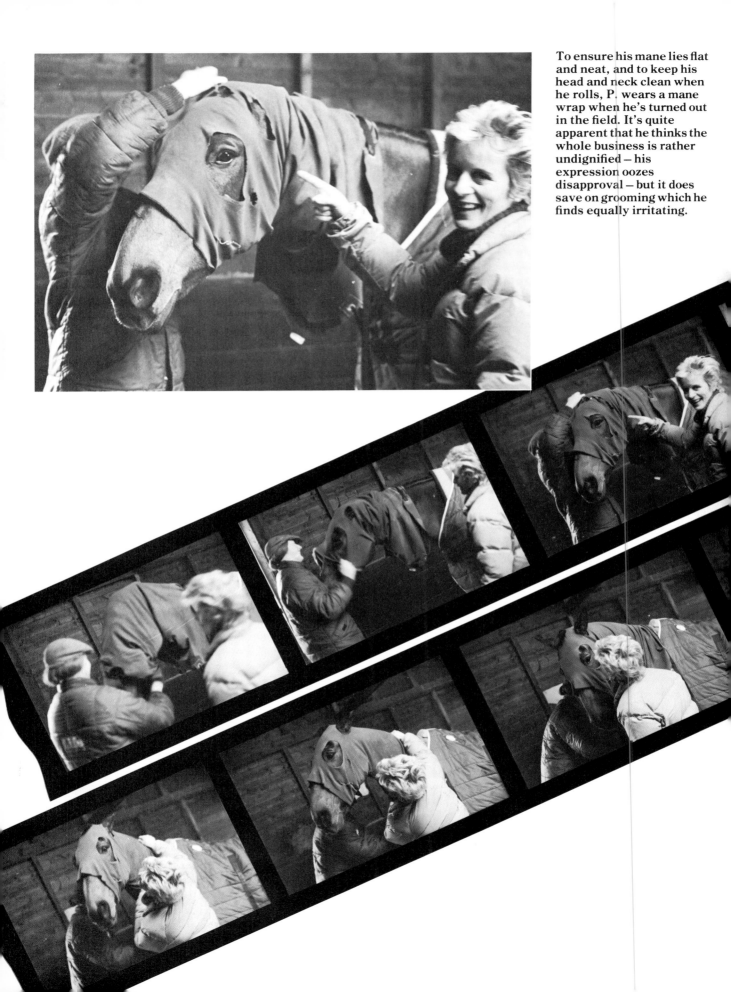

To ensure his mane lies flat and neat, and to keep his head and neck clean when he rolls, P. wears a mane wrap when he's turned out in the field. It's quite apparent that he thinks the whole business is rather undignified – his expression oozes disapproval – but it does save on grooming which he finds equally irritating.

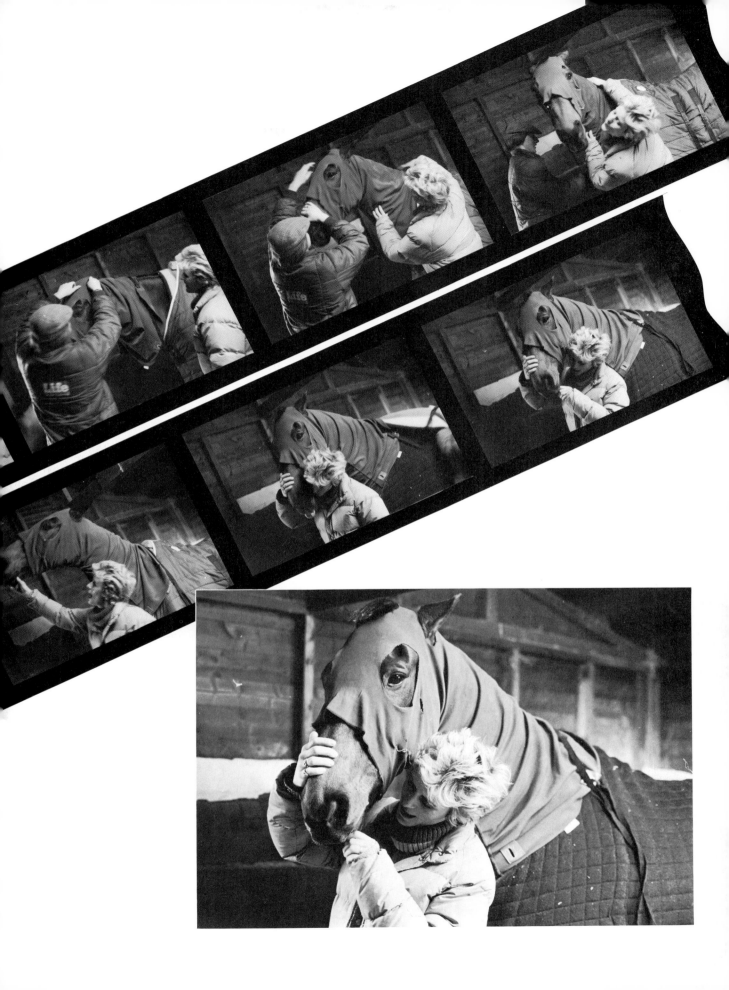

Heading for the field,
above, Elaine and P. step
out briskly.

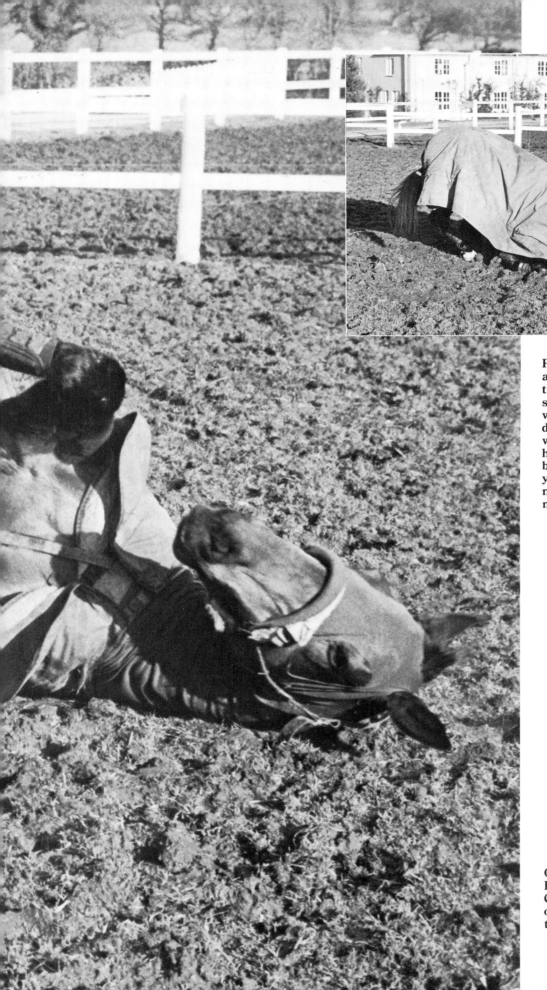

Priceless loves to roll and always makes a very thorough job of it: both sides and head and neck as well. His New Zealand rug doesn't just keep him warm, it saves Elaine hours of work. In the background one of the youngsters in a neighbouring paddock moves in for a closer look.

Overleaf: Winter sports. Priceless, left, and Night Cap are old friends and are often turned out in the field together to play.

 # The Perfect Event Horse...

'Priceless would never have been bought as a dressage horse – he wasn't designed for it, but thanks to careful training and his own 'Let's get on with it' personality he eventually produced some quite outstanding results. Sometimes his idea of 'getting on with it' had exciting consequences, but although that aspect of his character could be a drawback in his dressage work it was a positive advantage as far as his jumping was concerned. As long as we kept him thinking and amused he went on trying. You couldn't just say "Do it," to Priceless. If you did, he'd just turn round and say "Why?"'

Pat Manning
Dressage trainer

'He started his round in the World Championships swishing his tail and looking as if he wouldn't go a yard, but the further he went, the better he was – I think that's part of his character. He'll certainly go down as one of the all time greats.'

Richard Meade
Olympic Individual Gold Medallist 1972

'My most memorable image of Priceless was seeing him jump the Brandy Glass at Burghley in 1983. There was a gasp from everyone watching as Ginny chose the almost unjumpable route straight through on the left but P. popped through as though jumping three cavaletti, giving the impression that he had "walked the course" himself and studied it in precise detail. He made it all look so easy.

Mary Gordon Watson
World Champion 1970

I've always called Priceless the "troop horse with ideas above his station" because of his rather pony-like approach to life. When I was Commanding Officer of the King's Troop I used to threaten that if he ever stopped, I'd hog his mane and put him to pulling a gun. Of course he's never stopped and the Troop is poorer for that!
I'd always ask Ginny to go first on a team because I was convinced that Priceless would never be surprised by what he met. Nothing ever seemed to worry him. He was totally reliable and he always trotted up sound. I'm an unashamed fan.

Malcolm Wallace
Chef d'Equipe for the British team

'I actually thought Priceless was rather a cobby little fellow when I first saw him. He was very nice and jumped very well but at the time I didn't think much more about him. I certainly didn't imagine that he would turn out to be the sort of hero he has proved to be.

Then he went to the European Championships in Denmark in 1981. He wasn't terribly fast but he went clear, and to chart a course in that way is pretty impressive. That's when I first noticed his star quality.

He is a totally genuine horse. He quite obviously has a character, and you can't tell him what to do, but great horses are like that. He's very independent, and with the wrong rider he could easily have got extremely browned off, but Ginny has been clever enough to form the ability to coax that extra brilliance out of him. Partnerships like that usually only happen once in a lifetime.'

Lucinda Green
World Champion 1982

'Some of us have been fortunate enough to follow the career of a horse which will, without a doubt, be numbered among the world's greatest eventers, ably ridden by a remarkably talented jockey.

It is important for an event horse to do well in the dressage phase of a competition, as quite a number of the best competitors add no further penalties to their dressage scores during the cross-country or show jumping phases. I have seen Priceless in this position on many occasions.

Thanks to Ginny's sympathy and tact he really tried hard and performed accurate, pleasing tests which usually earned him good marks. Priceless could hold his own in the best company.'

Dinah Brocklehurst
FEI Three-Day Event dressage judge

'Priceless loved eventing as much as Ginny does. I think he made that obvious at Gawler when he was really quite naughty at the start of the cross-country. At the first fence he took off in the wrong place: banked it instead of going over the top and then bucked on the other side – but he was only taking the mick! He's a crafty old devil and loves fooling around but he would never be too scatty; he has enough common sense to cope with difficult problems. You could trust him completely to do his job.

He didn't look a world beater, or even a fast galloper, but he is when it comes to it. He's also a lovely person with a lot of character, like so many horses that do well. He does everything slightly tongue in cheek as if to say: "Don't push me too far!" He enjoyed cross-country, his dressage was good and he would produce a copy book show jumping round every time. The perfect event horse.'

Lorna Clarke
British team member

'On the day of the cross-country at the Los Angeles Olympics, Ginny and Priceless set off early. I wanted a shot of them jumping the Crescent Oxer which I knew could be spectacular if – as Dot had told me – they took the direct route through the centre. If they had decided to choose the easy way round the side I would have missed my picture altogether. It was a gamble, especially as no one before them took the central route and a lot of the riders seemed to be making heavy weather of the course. The gloomy predictions that no one would go clear seemed to have a ring of truth. Then Priceless and Ginny appeared, heading straight for the centre of the oxer. It was the most enormous fence, but they just sailed over it. As they carried on round the course I could hear the commentator saying: "Clear, clear, clear," and it was as if a cloud had lifted.'

Kit Houghton
Equestrian photographer

'He's a bit of a legend really. I'd read and heard a lot about him before I ever saw him but it wasn't until the team started training together for the 1984 Olympics that I realised quite how brilliant he was. In the flesh he looks like a very large pony, and when he wasn't fit you might have wondered whether he'd be capable of Three-Day eventing. Once you study him in action though, he leaves you in no doubt. Throughout the team training he stood out above the rest. He did everything that bit better. He excelled in everything he did, particularly when he had an audience. He always thought he was special and he was jolly well right!

Ian Stark
British team member

'Priceless is a bit of a prima donna and he likes to be allowed to feel that he's doing things himself. Ginny says that riding him is like switching to auto-pilot, but a rider who didn't understand him as she does would never do so well. She loves him dearly and has great faith in him. All the way round a cross-country course she'd be telling him he was a good boy and patting him. Priceless loved that, and the more she praised him the more he liked it!

He's a horse who will definitely rise to occasions. On the last day of a big Three-Day Event, when everything might depend on him jumping clear, I've seen him kick a practice fence down outside, just to make Ginny think: Help! But then he'd go into the ring, tuck his feet up and try his heart out.'

Lady Hugh Russell
Cross-country trainer

'Ginny once described to me the difference between her two horses, Priceless and Night Cap. "Priceless is a survivor," she said, "and I know that in looking after himself he will take care of me."

Since then, as a reporter at nearly all the pair's major challenges, I have never been in any doubt that Ginny and Priceless would prove to be totally dependable members of the team, guaranteed to give a good performance at all stages of the competition, whatever the conditions.

One particular memory which stands out for me, was their superlative cross-country ride at Badminton in 1985, the year they won. Priceless seemed inspired. It had been sleeting, and conditions were not ideal, but he devoured the ground relentlessly, seeming to float over the massive obstacles in his path as if he hardly noticed them – for all the world as if he had heard the fairies summoning him on to the finish.'

Jane Pontifex
Equestrian journalist

'The reason that companies such as British National Life undertake a long-term sponsorship commitment are myriad, and bonus benefits are rare. But with us Priceless was without doubt one of those bonuses. Undoubtedly aware of his own uniqueness, he impressed his personality upon anyone that came in touch with him.

At the official opening of our new offices in 1984 his "cutting the ribbon" (biting a suspended carrot) assumed a significance amongst staff and the media that could not have been more effective if it had been scripted and rehearsed. Years later people still remember "the day they met Priceless".

Like Foxhunter the name of Priceless will live on; in the opinion of his sponsors never was a horse more aptly named.'

Valerie Gates
British National Life, sponsors of the Holgate team

'I thought he looked a bit bored at Gawler, but then I realised that he just had a wonderfully laid back attitude. What impressed me most was the perfect rapport he had with Ginny: a total trust between them which is quite rare. On the show jumping day one really felt from just looking at him that he wouldn't let anyone down – he would go clean.'

Eileen Thomas
Executive Director, United States Combined Training Association

'P. was a loner and he hated my 'Polo parties' – the name given to my regular athletic jumping sessions – which most horses enjoyed. But once he got in the ring he was transformed. The bigger the fences and more important the occasion, the better he would jump.

There was just one time when P. had to knuckle down and work in the grid. Before the team concentration at Wylye, prior to Gawler, he had developed a potentially dangerous tendency to drift to the left over fences. Ginny was at her wit's end, so instead of excusing him the full grid workout as we were apt to do, we took him through the complete session. In the course of it, one particular exercise made him pay attention and correct himself and, as a result, put him back on the straight and narrow again!

I always felt it a great privilege to work with Ginny and Priceless. My aim, as trainer, is to create a total oneness between horse and rider on all levels: physically, mentally, emotionally and spiritually. G. and P.'s love for each other was not mere sentiment. It was a bond between them that permeated and strengthened their every thought and action, and gave them a drive and an energy which seemed almost divine. They were so totally in harmony, in rhythm and in tune with each other that there seemed to be something greater still reflected in their relationship. A universal harmony, a hint of the unity of all creation. Surely the art of true horse-man-ship.'

Pat Burgess
Show jumping trainer

Index

Illustration credits

Black and white photographs
Kit Houghton: pages 9 (top and bottom), 10, 11, 13, 14, (right), 15, 18 (bottom), 19, 22, 25 (middle), 27, 34, 40, 41, 42, 43, 45, 47, 48, 49, 60, 64, (bottom), 68, 76, 78, 79, 80, 81, 82, 83, 84, 85, 86, 87, 92, 93
Stuart Newsham: pages 4, 20, 21, 25 (bottom), 51, 53, 54, 55, 56, 57, 61, 62, 63, 66
Jim Meads: pages 18 (middle), 28, 30, 37, 38, 64 (top), 69
Edward Farmer: pages 25 (top), 36 (left), 46
Martin Dalby: pages 73 (bottom), 74, 75
Barn Owl: pages 65, 88
Trevor Meeks: pages 70, 72
Steve Yarnell: pages 16, 58
Albert Adams: 73; Ross Campbell: 8; Photo Czerny: 33; Findlay Davidson: 67; David Knowles: 12

Colour plates
Cover and frontispiece: Kit Houghton; between pages 32, 33: Kit Houghton, Bob Langrish, Findlay Davidson; between pages 48, 49: Kit Houghton, Associated Sports, Allsport; between pages 64, 65: Stuart Newsham, Steve Yarnell, Kit Houghton; between pages 80, 81: Kit Houghton

Line drawings
Eddie Poulton page 26; Miss F. H. Clough by permission of Burghley Horse Trials pages 29, 39